Living Your Best Compliance Life:

65 HACKS & CHEAT CODES TO LEVEL UP YOUR ETHICS & COMPLIANCE PROGRAM

by MARY SHIRLEY

Living Your Best Compliance Life: 65 Hacks & Cheat Codes to Level Up Your Ethics & Compliance Program is published by CCI Press, an imprint of CCI Media Group, Fort Worth, Texas

Copyright © 2023 by Mary Shirley

ISBN: 978-1-7350285-5-2

Editors: Jennifer L. Gaskin and Emily Ellis

Designers: Jennifer L. Gaskin and Luis Martinez

Author photo: Stephanie Sinclair Howard

CCI Media Group

www.corporatecomplianceinsights.com

CCI Press is the publishing imprint of CCI Media Group,
parent company of Corporate Compliance Insights (CCI).
CCI is the web's premier independent, global source of
news and opinion for compliance, ethics, risk and audit.
Founded in 2010, CCI provides a knowledge-sharing forum
and publishing platform for established and emerging
voices in compliance and ethics and is a recognized creator,
publisher and syndication source for editorial and multime-
dia content for today's compliance professional.

This book is for those with
good hearts, and especially the
kindhearted underdogs.

CONTENTS

CONTENTS

ACKNOWLEDGMENTS

Much of the drafting of this book coincided with a personal endeavor to obtain a green card, also known as permanent residency in the United States. These dual workstreams were hard going at times, and fortunately for me, there was no end to the varying support I received for both efforts. My heartfelt thanks goes out to every individual who assisted me in any capacity during this time period. I felt you in my corner, your love, your hope for the best for me and this book, every step of the way.

To those named in the book alongside your ideas, thank you for caring about your stakeholders and bringing the very important work we do to life. I am so grateful to you for allowing me to showcase your innovations and creativity by way of this platform. It was a pleasure to work with you and highlight your brilliance.

To the colleagues who indulged me in substantive conversation as a form of research to help inspire and draw out my own ideas, thank you for being so giving of your time, belief in me to succeed and encouragement. Fred Stratmann, Steven Gyeszly, Cynthia Morrison, Monica Reinmiller Lopez, Melanie Sponholz, Donna Schneider, Matt Kelly, Al Gagne, Greg Brower, Ellen Hunt, Lisa Beth Lentini Walker and Jacki Cheslow.

To Tom Fox, for teaching me so much about the fundamentals of compliance before I knew him and always being willing to mentor and look out for me since I met him. Tom, you are my compliance MVP.

To Jared Knapp, for encouraging this book before I even knew what it was going to be about.

To Lisa Fine, my podcast wife, for the teamwork, care and loyalty in tough times.

To my parents, thank you for absolutely everything. You have given me the sun, the moon and the stars. There is no way that I can ever repay it, but know that I am grateful for every sacrifice, for teaching Kieran and me about the most important things in life, all of your hard work and all of the love and care.

This is a last but by no means least if ever there was one: Sarah Hadden, the head of Corporate Compliance Insights and CCI Press, the person who brought us this book. For making me a real, actual, legitimate author. THANK YOU!

INTRODUCTION

Ethics and compliance programs are constantly evolving. As a profession, we have had to adjust from being regulatory compliance professionals, operating under rules-based programs and resembling sheriffs, to ethical and (often) moral guardians of our companies, operating under values-based programs as business enablers.

We've had to lean on our interpersonal skills as a way to make the medicine go down easier. We aim to shed the "sheriff" reputation and be seen as true enablers of business, offering an ethics function that should be viewed as a competitive advantage.

We try to shift focus from the fact that we are a cost center, not a revenue earner and emphasize instead that we're a revenue/reputation preservation and protection department.

All the while, our scope and necessary skill set constantly grows. Our relevant subject matter has been branching into various areas like data privacy, data security, ESG, modern slavery and human trafficking, #metoo, artificial intelligence regulation, and so on, depending on how your organization is classifying risk. Sometimes the chief compliance officer takes on the entire portfolio of enterprise risk management in addition to ethics and compliance risks.

We are compelled to learn new areas and expand our subject matter expertise on an ongoing basis, closely tracking the evolution of our field.

We have been striving toward making the shift to Compliance 2.0 for several years, and now Compliance 3.0 is being bandied about, encapsulating features like data analytics, behavioral science and AI as new tools to guide us in reaching the next frontier, among other advancements in the field. And who knows what more is around the corner, waiting to change our landscape next? Our dynamics, circumstances and environment are constantly changing.

I wanted to provide compliance practitioners with ideas and inspiration that allow you to continue to build the ship while sailing it, to strive for a better and more effective program while the field advances and morphs around us.

This book is not about using fancy new tools and approaches — there are plenty of vendors happy to take your call and tell you about their solutions if that is what you are looking for. It is about your everyday compliance practitioner without access to unlimited resources or unlimited budget and who possesses a typical compliance skill set, looking to make a difference and advance their program without overreliance on specialist, and oftentimes rather pricey, service providers.

It is like a recipe book for home-cooked meals, and you are MacGyver, following the guide with the tools you have at hand.

It's important to not get complacent with your program, especially if your company has completed a corporate integrity agreement or monitorship in the past. The same standards that got you there years ago are part of continuously moving goal posts. It is incumbent on us to keep innovating and keep the program fresh for our colleagues to help avoid compliance fatigue setting in or, even worse, ineffectiveness.

That's why this book was written. To help give a starting point and some actionable ideas to compliance professionals who want to keep changing things up, continuously improve and provide a program that stimulates the learning experience for colleagues.

> **"Even if you're on the right track, you'll get run over if you just sit there."**
>
> — Will Rogers

We'll walk through a treasure trove of curated ideas for you to try in your own program. There is a time and a place for ruminating about theory, the academic side of compliance and government expectations, to be sure. But I believe where real added value exists for compliance practitioners is when we can share concrete ideas and takeaways with each other. That includes detailed examples and ideas that allow us to follow in each other's footsteps and be equipped to take immediate action, not just be inspired and agree with each other.

Beyond the examples and activities within this book, you will likely think of ways to build on the initiatives described here or tailor them and, ideally, make them even better, more scalable and more impactful. Hopefully you will be inspired to create more of your own initiatives and share them with the ethics and compliance community yourself: Think about writing an article or speaking at a conference to share your novel approach. If you've mused writing or speaking for the first time, please take this as a sign that you should make the leap.

Not all ideas will work for your current circumstances; it's unlikely that the average compliance officer will be able to effectively implement every single idea outlined here, and that's to be expected. Perhaps the level of maturity of your compliance program currently precludes you from venturing to try certain ideas. Perhaps the fact you are a compliance department of one means you're not able to implement some of these hacks and tips. Think of this book like a menu and order the items that you're hungry for (and can achieve) in the near-term. Disregard for now what does not apply to your status quo and consider revisiting ideas that may work for your future role and circumstances.

Before you commence this journey, you may wish to measure the impact your efforts have on the business and your team scores in your organization's employee engagement survey. Try setting a goal to implement one idea per month, mapping out a plan for the year. Before you begin, consider issuing a culture of integrity survey that will be your baseline for measuring current attitudes toward your compliance program and the department itself. After twelve to twenty-four months, issue the survey again and look for positive change to your culture of integrity and mentions of the activities you have launched. Favorable results from your tracking and measurement can then be used for performance review and other self-promotional opportunities to demonstrate the company's return on investment in hiring you.

As they say, shoot for the moon, and if you miss, you'll land among the stars.

PROGRAM ASSESSMENT

Before a doctor can cure you, they first have to diagnose you. The same is true of your compliance program. Having deep knowledge of how well your program is already working will help you understand which of these hacks and cheat codes are right for you. And remember: Assessment is a continuous process, as you always want to keep leveling up.

Recognize the Weakness of Centralized Compliance Program Controls

When we identify a control failure or some other gap in our compliance program, it can be tempting to jump on the immediate issue at hand and remediate the problem in the region/business unit within which it occurred, log that task as complete and move on with your life.

However, if an issue occurs in one area of the business, there's a good chance that vulnerability could be penetrated in another area of the business.

The Eli Lilly FCPA case makes for very interesting reading about how four bribery schemes occurred across one multinational organization in four countries. Make sure that when addressing specific issues that have occurred, you consider where else in your program there might be an issue. Do some controls testing and review transactions elsewhere that may reveal more systemic issues and wider internal controls system failures. Be communicative with compliance officers elsewhere in the business if you identify an issue that has occurred that may be problematic for them under their portfolio — either now or in the future.

> **Pro tip:** Ask centralized functions with broad oversight into various areas of the business, such as the investigations or the internal audit team (ideally both if you can), to share overarching patterns with you about issues they're spotting in multiple regions. This is an opportunity to gain insight into systemic issues and tap into real-life scenarios to use in your training (more on training later).

Query Whether Existing Software Might Do the Job of Vendor Software

In my subject matter expert chats for this book, I spoke with a compliance practitioner who told me about how she uses the call intake service of her hotline provider but doesn't use their case management system for her investigation case tracking; rather, she uses existing software her company already had.

In addition to the money savings of taking this tack, I see another benefit of doing this: She retains better control of sensitive data. If the third-party provider suffers a data breach, she has less information outside of her own control that could be exposed.

This idea can be applied to all areas of your compliance program. It's worth auditing the various vendors and services you use, itemizing the specific jobs they and their software do for you, and then having a meeting with your IT department to discuss whether any of the vendor solutions might be replaced by tools the company has already invested in for another purpose.

Use Your Compliance Week or Compliance Fair as a Two-Way Feedback Mechanism and Qualitative Data Analytics Opportunity

I bet you already have a fancy risk assessment and have been utilizing culture-of-compliance/culture-of-integrity surveys to get feedback from your business for quite some time now — enough to see year-on-year trends, even.

These surveys and assessments certainly have their place: They're a fantastic way to measure your culture of integrity and signal gaps and areas of opportunity. The downside, however, is that they can be time-consuming to implement and analyze, and, of course, they require buy-in from the business.

I recommend a "pulse check" at an annual compliance week event, in which the company dedicates a week of focus on the compliance function and program and incorporates fun activities and events, such as a compliance fair, in the festivities.

The benefit of a pulse check at an annual compliance event is that it's an immediate, focused indicator of what you need to know. The best part: You don't need to persuade your colleagues to participate. They will be literally lining up to give you juicy information to improve and better direct your compliance program efforts. Because playing games at events like this doesn't feel as serious as, say, a risk assessment interview, staff may give more candid feedback, which can be very reliable for actioning future initiatives.

So, how do we do this?

Depending on what information you're seeking and how you intend to use it, there are several ways to use an annual compliance event to inform your upcoming efforts and attention.

Where possible, keep it themed. One year, we did a carnival theme; another year, the theme was rodeo. At each event, there were several activities tied to the theme, and the following feedback mechanisms were woven into those activities:

To determine whether you're succeeding as a business partner and true enabler of business, set up a simple easel with paper and markers or a whiteboard and ask staff to write the one word that comes to mind when they hear "compliance."

This will give you an idea of staff perceptions, and you can hand out candy, stickers or a compliance-related, company branded item in conjunction with collecting this feedback ("Cheers to Compliance!" on mugs, for example). Of course, nothing so lavish as to influence the comments!

Similarly if you're looking for general feedback, set up the easel and ask, "How can we serve you better?"

A lot of the time, the feedback coming in will be on the success of your education program and ideas for improving it; this can be pretty handy, as it doesn't make sense to roll out a whole culture-of-integrity survey just to get feedback on how the program is being received. You'll also get some good "food for thought" feedback, which can be put on the agenda for your next department meeting. There is a lot of room for flexibility in what you can ask to learn about how your compliance program is being received.

For more focused inquiries, such as identifying whether your annual training content has stuck five months on, or whether you need to go back to basics, try quiz-related activities. Examples include:

- A Jeopardy-style contest is great for staff unable to attend in-person activities. Review your annual training and select key takeaways, then position them as quiz questions for your game.

- Lucky draw prizes. These can be relatively inexpensive — we bought Amazon Echo Dots on sale one year and used them as giveaways and got a lot of feedback about how the prizes were cool. (Wow! They're practically saying we in compliance are cool!)

- Create a ring-toss game in which players must correctly answer compliance quiz questions to earn rings to throw.

- One year we featured a spin-the-wheel game with the seven elements of an effective compliance program on each sector and relevant questions for each.

To test whether you are all set on the basics and to identify whether there are some gaps yet to be bridged, try quiz questions with the most basic answers you can think of. These should be questions you think almost all staff will know the answer to. For instance, "who is the chief compliance officer?" "What is the compliance hotline?" "Where can you access the code of conduct?" and so on. I guarantee you'll be so shocked with some of these answers that you'll have a great starting point for a gap analysis after just a few dozen people have played the game. This exercise can be truly humbling, but it's better you know about the gaps and be well-positioned to address low-hanging fruit.

Using the data ...

These temperature checks are certainly not designed to replace aspects of your compliance program, such as your risk assessment. They can, however, be helpful in understanding how to address gaps or increase communication with your business, including as a qualitative data analytics opportunity.

When we think of data analytics, it can be tempting to think about this requirement in terms of assessing quantitative data or information that your company has gathered in terms of, for example, sales figures, expense claims and associated trends. But that's not the only important information a compliance department has access to that can enhance a program per the expectations re-emphasized in the Department of Justice (DOJ) guidance from June 2020.

You may assume your compliance program excels in certain areas that a pulse check indicates are sorely in need of improvement — whether using a different format to cover annual training topics that team members have recently reviewed but not retained, creating a podcast interview or new blog series with your CCO and communicating with the business through methods they'll actually engage with.

Pulse checks can be sobering activities, but the kind of information they can provide is key to ensuring you have more than a paper program, that you're in touch with your key constituents and that you're intent on being a good business partner.

Plus, you'll be collecting this data from colleagues in a fun environment, where they're not feeling scrutinized or in trouble for giving the "wrong" answers, and you get immediate feedback from colleagues who are excited about participating.

The Unsolicited Feedback Key Performance Indicator (KPI)

The compliance community is very passionate about discussing what KPIs they consider are folly and don't actually tell us anything valuable.

The old favorite to criticize is the lack of utility in tracking training completion rates for an organization, for example, because all that really tells us is that someone sat in our presence for a specified period of time (not necessarily paying attention or learning anything) or clicked through a specified number of pages (not necessarily paying attention or learning anything). A better measure, according to these critics, is gauging the level of absorption by testing knowledge some time after training has taken place to see if the learning has stuck.

I would argue that tracking completion of compliance training is also a worthy KPI, not because of what it is in and of itself, but because if we considered the alternative, which is not caring about whether people complete compliance training at all, well, that is a fairly heinous place to be, and I can't imagine such a lackadaisical approach would be encouraged by regulators. Therefore, my view is to note the limitations of what completion rates tell you, additionally measure absorption of learning objectives in a way you see fit to indicate whether your training is working and continue to encourage completion of training, because we do care that it gets done.

Pro tip: Consider compiling unsolicited feedback in one team-wide repository. This will let you look out for trends and take a more holistic view about the types of feedback you're getting. And it will give you documentary evidence come performance review time or in opportune moments to broadcast that the compliance department is showing a return on investment by way of stakeholder reception.

But that's not all we should be doing. A not-so-conventional way we can get an idea as to the effectiveness of our compliance program, including training, is by the level of unsolicited positive feedback we receive. Unforced, wholly volunteered information is a wonderfully genuine sign of how we are being received by our stakeholders.

People are often eager to please executives, and no one wants to look like they disregard ethics and compliance, even if they're a detractor. So you don't want to see a brand-new CCO enthusiastically asking colleagues about how much they're enjoying this year's Compliance Week, receive the response they want to hear, then report back to the executive leadership team that the first Compliance Week held on their watch was the best one ever.

I remember someone catching up to a former CCO of mine, Lisa Estrada, to volunteer the information that it was the most fun week they had working at the company. That's a more reliable assessment because someone went out of their way to say, "Hey, I'm participating in your activities and I love them!"

I would be so bold as to suggest that even constructive criticism, thoughtfully proffered, is a positive sign, too: It shows that colleagues care enough to engage with you and consider that it's worth their time to share their thoughts because they think you'll listen — and that is important information. That they view you as approach-able and willing to listen is a great sign you're doing something right!

A word of caution is to pay atten-tion to what the feedback is really saying. For example, an overly abbreviated training might be considered "good" training by a

Pro tip: Send the elevator back down and be mindful about calling out the successes and strengths of your colleagues throughout the year, both internal and external, to help their unsolicited positive feedback KPIs.

person who dreads taking training, but that speaks to their relief in having to pay attention only to scant messaging and investing little time rather than whether the training was meaningful, effective or helped them to do their job better.

Having this as a known, official KPI within the team can be easy to game; for example, a team member eager to check the box of this KPI might enlist a friend within the organization to send them a positive feedback message that has been crafted solely to hit the KPI and isn't genuine. So, it may be best left as a private, personal KPI you hold for yourself to be a reassuring pat on the back that you and your team are on the right track.

Keep a Travel Playbook

Though many good things have come from the pandemic, one of the less desirable for compliance officers, in my opinion, is that many folks governing budgets will point to the "shelter-in-place" years as an argument that we can get by without needing to travel. I'd argue the key words there are "get by" — we were, indeed, surviving, but were we thriving and effective?

Simon Sinek repeatedly makes the point in *Leaders Eat Last* that no matter how much technology advances, there is no substitute for the benefits of humans connecting in person. Yes, video conferences are a way to communicate information "face to face." And yes, picking up the telephone can defuse fractious discussions via email. But there undeniably is something about meeting in person that helps cement the human bond and trust between colleagues.

To help demonstrate the return on investment of his team's travel, Louis Sapirman, a veteran CCO, has come up with a travel playbook in which the team carefully documents details of each trip and what the benefit was for the company of each one.

Think of applying this to other areas of your compliance program, at least until we successfully manage to rename our departments to the Revenue/Reputation Protection and Preservation Department!

Get Real When it Comes to Current Initiatives

Louis Sapirman has a brilliantly simple idea for understanding whether you're hitting the "Seven Elements of a Compliance Program" as outlined by the U.S. Sentencing Guidelines for Organizations and other program aspects you aim to satisfy, such as culture of integrity, behavioral science, data analytics/AI, tone from the top (which is obliquely referenced by the UK's Ministry of Justice) or other features of your program.

To implement Louis' idea, set up and complete a simple table. Down the left axis, list all the elements of a compliance program you want to be addressing. On the right axis, list all of the initiatives and tools you have in place to satisfy each. Ideally, you want to see a number of attempts to address each element. As you list each initiative, don't just blindly slap it on the table. Ask yourself, for continuous monitoring, review and improvement purposes, does this activity:

1. Actually address the element?

2. Have sufficient tweaking done to it every so often to be fresh? (Review and monitor always, folks.)

3. Work better than any alternatives that may have arisen since we first started doing it?

Here is an example of what this may look like, and remember: It's worth reviewing this table and asking yourself the honest monitoring questions every year or two.

65 HACKS + CHEAT CODES TO LEVEL UP YOUR ETHICS + COMPLIANCE PROGRAM

INITIATIVES TO ADDRESS COMPLIANCE PROGRAM ELEMENTS

Print and fill this table in. For example, under "Tone from the top," one company listed: Executives teaching learning objectives in training, CEO coming up with initiatives for program and taking responsibility for implementation and management doing a "Compliance Minute" at the beginning of every meeting.

Element of program	Initiatives in place		
Tone from the top			
Written policies & procedures			

SCAN THIS QR CODE TO DOWNLOAD + PRINT THE FULL VERSION

You will likely want to populate the table proportionately depending on what is important to you based on various sources of guidance that apply to your company and program, both U.S. and international. (As a Kiwi, I'll be the first to say that for many of us, the United States is international; however, I'm giving the DOJ's guidance some deference here given the U.S. is essentially the motherland for anti-corruption enforcement, and it's very likely that the vast majority of folks reading this book are American.)

Create a Compliance Shared Service Center

Larger organizations have been leveraging shared service centers for quite some time. Designed to centralize certain "back office" functions in support of the broader company, such as finance, human resources, IT and (perhaps best known) customer support, shared service centers are a mature operation today. So why not apply the same type of model to an effort like compliance?

That is a question that Christopher Annand, ethics and compliance director at Cargill, asked himself early in his career when working with a financial services corporation that had opened a center for other functions and had room to experiment with a smaller team. After finding success with the first attempt, Christopher was presented the opportunity to expand the concept when he accepted a larger role with a major agricultural and food production company.

With the chance to enhance his prior model, Christopher started his new effort with the same first step — identifying what compliance activities and tasks would benefit the most from the shared services model. To be considered, the work would need to meet a set of criteria:

- Was the work/activity standardized and not subject to customization?
- Was the work/activity able to follow a repeatable process that could be easily trained?
- Would the work/activity generate metrics that could be used to show efficiency or cost-reduction gains?
- Were there advantages to having the work/activity performed in a different geography than the U.S. headquarters, where compliance leadership was based?

From this set of questions, certain activities quickly rose for consideration, such as compliance training deployments, policy management, due diligence activities and simple employee support with questions about compliance requirements and procedures. Even more complex compliance actions often were found to have portions of their process that could benefit from a shared services approach. For example, while it might not be practical to have the entire management of a company's employee whistleblower hotline within a shared services team, initial triage of submissions and quality control of their assignment to investigators was certainly an option.

Once the activities had been identified and grouped into buckets that could become a role description, Christopher was then able to work with his global HR department to assess talent pools in the locations where his company currently operated centers. Sourcing talent was not difficult; Christopher knew that financial service companies had begun moving their anti-money laundering compliance operations to shared service centers, which provided a good pool of talent that would understand basic compliance concepts that he could train his broader procedures around. Additionally, because people in these roles often were limited to performing only a small set of tasks, Christopher's larger and more diversified roles would likely be attractive.

Within 12 months of launching the effort at his current company, Christopher was able to build a team of eight compliance analysts in a center based in Bengaluru (Bangalore), India. Only six months later, he expanded his team into a second location with six analysts in San José, Costa Rica. Having a team across two major regions not only allowed for more targeted compliance support by geography, but also provided the ability to have work begun in one location and then continued and completed in another. That allowed Christopher to leverage the time zone difference between his teams rather than seeing it as a liability.

One of the greatest benefits that Christopher has seen from this model is the ability for these teams to serve as talent pools for the larger compliance department. Some employees who started at the analyst level now manage larger portions of the program themselves, having built their experience through Christopher's teams. And the initial set of activities and services has grown as well, where almost every portion of the global compliance framework has an element supported through shared services. While expanding a compliance team through a shared services operation is not without cost, Christopher was able to achieve significant labor arbitrage while offering attractive roles with opportunities for career advancement within the centers — sometimes at almost a 75% savings compared with similar roles based in the United States or other locations.

Christopher acknowledged that not every company has the ability to employ a shared services strategy and that it would be highly unusual for a compliance department to be the first function to launch a center on its own. However, for those companies that have adopted the model with the more traditional functions, he believes there can be exciting opportunities to grow a compliance program at a faster speed and lower cost by asking the question, "Why not compliance?"

TEAM-BUILDING

Going around the room saying
something interesting about yourself
is certainly one way to build a spirit
of camaraderie in your organization.
But is that really why you're reading
this book? Focus on team-building at
all levels, both inside and outside the
organization.

Create a Compliance Program Advisory Board

Advisory boards are a form of strategic, external consultancy and input sought by organizations. They can help you navigate challenges and provide much-needed guidance to steer initiatives and best serve your stakeholders.

Some colleagues are particularly interested in ethics and compliance even though they don't work in the function. Others want the ability to influence the program, and having their voice heard early in the process can help with buy-in and understanding from compliance. They might caution you about a problem they see that simply is not within the line of sight of a compliance officer and allow you to adapt appropriately before rollout.

Advertise the opportunity to sit on the Compliance Program Advisory Board (a more catchy and alluring name for your advisory board is something to work on!), and collect volunteers who will happily commit to giving you feedback and the chance to pilot ideas and new initiatives with them.

Pro tip:
This idea is particularly useful if you do not have a formal compliance champion/ ambassador program established within your organization — speaking of which …

Incorporate an Air of Prestige Around Compliance Champions

Anointing compliance champions is based on the reality that compliance officers can't be everywhere at once, especially in large, sprawling organizations where there may be small clusters of staff dotted in remote regions of the world.

To combat this, many companies deploy ambassadors, or compliance champions, who help clarify compliance questions on the ground. They may hype up the program, act as liaisons, carry out quick translations into a local language, share feedback with headquarters or regional compliance and so on. They help you stay better connected to the business and amplify your voice with theirs — one that is likely better known to the business and well-respected in the local organization.

Chief Compliance Officer Beth Colling has spoken about the success of the compliance champion initiative within CDM Smith, a Boston-based construction and engineering firm. What CDM Smith does differently is that the role of compliance champion is one that has a reputation in the company for being a special, well-deserved opportunity and leadership aspiration. At CDM Smith, it is an honor to be selected for and carry out this role.

Think about what other aspects of your program could be elevated to an extraordinary position of responsibility in which it's a privilege and reward to participate. Tone from the top is critical for making this idea a success. Ask your management what ideas they have to make the responsibility a sought-after and desirable one. It need not necessarily come with extra compensation — though, of course, that is an option to consider.

Time the Release of a Compliance Routine Initiative with Your Compliance Week or Compliance Fair

Incorporating some of your training initiatives, launch of your revised code of conduct or other projects perceived as less joyous by our stakeholders into compliance-focused events helps to carry the theme of the week and ties in something that, unfortunately, is often considered a chore with more enjoyable activities, thereby replacing a negative association with a positive one.

Pro tip: Increase the interest levels of colleagues and draw out the competitive side of staff further by putting those who complete the training or acknowledge reviewing the new policy document by the due date in the drawing for a prize. Advertise this incentive as part of the week's festivities to create buzz.

Sponsorship Opportunities for Compliance Week or Compliance Fairs

Plant a seed for leaders to offer sponsorship of annual compliance week activities as a way for them to demonstrate commitment to ethics and integrity visibly, as well as help you stretch your presence, credibility and resources further.

You can offer varying levels of sponsorship and set dollar values for each, as with traditional event sponsorship, or a business unit could donate an iPad or something else as a prize for one of the contests. Make sure to make reference to the generous sponsorship and where it came from in your materials and announcements, as well as sending a thank-you note to acknowledge the leader's tone from the top. For example, a video game company provides an extra day off per quarter for their compliance champions to reward them for their additional services to the ethics and compliance function.

Share the Professional Development Love

Keep an eye out for complimentary conference and webinar offerings. Search for local roundtables or networking events to attend, too. Many law firms and compliance consultancies offer excellent sessions throughout the year. Sign up for relevant firm newsletters to get on their mailing lists and increase your chances of being invited to a local event.

It is tempting to assume free courses are inferior to conferences that come at a cost of registration, but if you compare the speaker lists, you'll see that the same speakers are often sharing their knowledge at both types of events.

Pro tip: Many of us think to share items of interest on an individual basis, especially with team leaders or peers within teams, but think about having a dedicated forum within your compliance department to share these events with colleagues so that you can take advantage of each other's networks. Share opportunities you see with your friends in compliance outside of your organization as well so they'll think of you when these events come across their desk.

Turn Innovating, Advancing Your Program or Proactive Problem-Solving Into a Concerted Compliance Team Effort

I'll be the first person to say "That meeting could have been an email." If it were socially acceptable to do so, I'd even consider wearing a T-shirt during office hours with that slogan emblazoned on the front of it as a just-in-time reminder.

Oh, how I despise wasting time and indulging people who like the sound of their own voice without adding any value. I will concede that meetings are, however, necessary from time to time and can be used as a way to dedicate focused time to improving your compliance program.

Another way to achieve the same goal can be to use your company's internal compliance summit and have each team present on how they addressed a problem, innovated creatively or improved the compliance program. Or bring a problem with a view to solving it with crowdsourcing by the end of the event.

It need not be a standing agenda item frequently, but consider if once a month or once a quarter might be appropriate.

Accelerating the Team Bonding Process in a Virtual Workplace Environment

I once moved from a regional role to an international compliance role within the same organization. Although the move was internal, my new team was composed of colleagues I didn't know very well or at all for the most part. I was conscious of the fact that when they applied to work at the company, they had made their decision to accept offers based on working for other supervisors — and then they got me.

I was domiciled on another continent, time zones away from my reports in the Frankfurt area. Even if I lived just down the road from the office, the raging pandemic meant we were confined to our homes in any event. I needed to replicate the getting-to-know-each-other and bonding that occurs organically by crossing paths in the office, at team lunches and after-work drinks.

I came up with a temporary slate of additional, virtual team get-togethers that focused on each team member, one at a time. In the lead-up to each person's focus session, they would share with everyone else what their favorite foods and drinks were and from that list, each member would select some of the preferred snacks to help get to know each other's tastes (literally, in this case) and give a party feel to the event.

One of my team members at the time, Jasper, is originally from the Netherlands. Jasper told us about Dutch chocolate sprinkles being one of his favorite treats, and I asked how to use them. (Apply liberally to any snack, it seems, is the way forward, in case you're curious.) Thanks to Amazon, I was able to join a celebration of Jasper with real-deal Dutch sprinkles. Armed with our food and drink, we engaged in an "Ask me anything" session and found that we very quickly learned more interesting things about each other in a short span of time compared with what you learn incidentally at after-work drinks.

I'm going to continue this approach when transitioning into new roles, even if I'm sitting in the same office as my new colleagues in the future. It was a great way to cement relationships, discover passions outside of work and learn about preferred working styles.

Sample working-style questions

How do you like to receive feedback?

How do you like to have appreciation shown to you? Public or private?

What's your communication style?

How do you work best under high-pressure situations?

What kind of support do you need from the team to be most effective at your job?

Don't lead a team yourself yet but like the sound of this? Suggest it to your boss and file it away for when you're a manager.

Sample personal questions

What 3-5 values guide you the most in your personal life?

Have you had another career before compliance? And/ or have you always wanted to work in compliance?

Do you lean more toward extroversion or introversion?

What motivates you?

What is on your bucket list?

What was your last dream that came true?

> **"The greatest good you can do for another is not just to share your riches but to reveal to him his own."**
>
> — Benjamin Disraeli

New hires joining your team (or you joining their team) isn't the only situation in which you can deploy such an exercise. To help increase morale in the team, for example, after there has been some friction or a when restructure is impending, try the maximizer exercise. Named for one of Gallup's Clifton-Strengths personas, this exercise encourages everyone to focus on their strengths, identifying them with the help of colleagues and working to take themselves from good to great. There is no dwelling on deficiencies here!

Ask each individual to drop a personal note to every other member of the team telling the recipient what their super-strengths are. The purpose is to allow team members to identify areas that they can explore further to truly excel and bring a sense of joy to each person who gets the feel-good factor of hearing what others love about them to build morale.

From a timing perspective, even with larger teams, this shouldn't take too much time out of your day — you should be able to shoot off a message in less than five minutes for each individual. For larger teams, you may wish to claim some time on calendars or do the exercise together in person as an activity at your compliance summit.

When I did this exercise with my team, I sent out my messages immediately just so everyone could envisage what the notes would look like.

One of my team members called me after she had received all of her amalgamated strengths and said she really wanted to thank me for this exercise. She told me it was something that truly lifted her spirits and gave her a positive feeling all day, and she was really glad we did it. So was I, not only to be brought a smile reading about what my team thought my strong points are but also after hearing the intended impact was felt by my team.

Maybe being saddled with me as a manager rather than chosen wasn't so bad …

Creating Cross-Functional Teams Within Your Compliance Department

Another Lisa Estrada gem that works particularly well in larger compliance functions is to build teams within teams. My specific example was creating a marketing team within the compliance department that worked on elements affecting department reputation, outreach/advocacy and awareness. A major project the marketing team was tasked with was the annual compliance week event. It also led the mission statement exercise described in another section.

The marketing team is but one focus area for a cross-pollinated team. You can also set up a committee that focuses on professional development opportunities for the department, such as arranging guest speakers, identifying and communicating about educational resources, coordinating the compendium of people and websites to follow, administering budget requests for conferences and obtaining opportunities for team members to speak at conferences, podcasts, webinars etc. Whatever you might need that could be a team work project, think about whether it warrants pulling together a cross-pollinated team.

Working groups on substantive matters can also be served by these groups. For example, a small, centralized training team might be supported by a wider group of compliance colleagues internationally outside of the team that functions as a training working group who act as liaisons with the local business lines.

While most people hate silos, the fact of the matter is that in large teams, especially geographically widespread ones, you don't always get exposure to every person in the department organically. Cross-functional teams can be an effective way to bring together colleagues whose paths do not naturally cross in their day-to-day work.

Include IT on Both Sides

Team-building doesn't just happen within your four walls. When starting a technology implementation, make sure to include a representative from your IT department as well as from the vendor's organization.

Importantly, make sure it's the right kind of expert on your side to ensure that there is value in this inclusion. Explain what you're trying to do in advance and have IT nominate their most appropriate person.

Marianne Ibrahim, a chief compliance officer in the oil and gas space, notes that IT experts working at service providers tend to be honest: They'll tell you up front if something can or can't be done, and their insights can be invaluable to your team — if you'll only ask.

Crash Some Parties

Walter Johnson is a quiet figure in the compliance space. As two introverts, he and I are able to talk forever in a one-on-one conversation. But put us in a bigger room of folks, especially with strangers, and we're a little more out of our element.

Despite that, we know that for compliance officers, it's incredibly important to build relationships and have allies all throughout the business, as well as to learn from those on the front lines exactly what it is that they do, to enable us to ask relevant questions and advise competently when the time comes.

In the book *How Women Rise* by Sally Helgesen and Marshall Goldsmith, the authors discuss that men are often better at prioritizing making connections and building relationships early in their tenure and women tend to focus on the substantive areas, potentially neglecting early relationship building.

Let's learn from Walter how we all can be better at doing this.

Walter has made it a priority and almost a challenge to have lunch with a new person in the organization each week. It need not be the team leader of that department, just someone who will become his contact in that area of the business going forward. His meet-ups are nothing fancy; they often occur at the cafeteria of his workplace, and Walter is always prepared to pay for his guest as the initiator of the meeting. He takes the time to learn about the person and what they do, asking smart, strategic questions to help gather information. Walter is a generous listener with a smile that never falters — it's easy to see how this can be a marvelous opportunity to really get to know his colleagues.

In the past, Walter has deployed his lunch break and keen interest in golf to create an opportunity to socialize and have colleagues opt into getting to know him, too. He has extended a regular invitation to staff to join him for some golf or tennis to combine work and leisure pursuits. Unlike old boys' club golfing events of the past, these events are inclusive and open to all who wish to participate.

He has also told me that he takes every opportunity he can to attend events he hears about in the organization and make a compliance appearance at all sorts of parties (as a fellow introvert, I am in admiration of him running toward events and not staying safe behind his desk, as I am fond of doing). "Mary, I've attended a lot of baby showers," he said with a chuckle and twinkle in his eye. And why not? What a gentle way to make acquaintance with unfamiliar faces in the business while celebrating important life events and showing that compliance cares.

Like with compliance week, the more we can get out there and be human in environments that are fun and positive, the more we build our reputation for being approachable and, well, human. Perhaps I might just move away from my desk for five minutes and join the party …

Legal and compliance expert Kevin Withane set an interesting goal in 2022 of having 100 meetings with colleagues, no set agenda in mind, just building relationships and bonds. A great challenge to try!

Invite Your CEO to Helm a Compliance Initiative

For the most part, we are expected to be the ones with all the ideas for our compliance programs, in addition to administering the program, but it doesn't have to be that way.

In fact, there are distinct benefits to passing the baton to someone else to take charge of compliance, even if only to spark an idea. Seeking the views of others early and often helps to insert diversity of thought into your compliance program, as we discuss in other areas of the book.

Ask your CEO to think about something they would like to implement as a contribution to the compliance program.

The former CEO of a multinational organization I worked for requested that the company show commitment to ethics and integrity by including a slide titled "We All Own Compliance" within every presentation, including when the subject matter of the presentation is not related to compliance.

This was a great initiative for the compliance team to build on, offering workshops for managers and other members of the business to coach them as they crafted a personal wardrobe of stories they could pull from for different occasions.

Perhaps unsurprisingly, the level of adoption and seriousness with which the business took this request was swift and strong. With the CEO releasing a compliance initiative, there was built-in tone from the top attached, and we in compliance just needed to support the initiative, lending follow-up help. What could your CEO do to help you gain traction in your program?

There is also scope for encouraging your CEO to talk about compliance in non-compliance forums. So often we see CEOs talking about core business strategy and current events on social media and in interviews, but they don't refer to ethics, compliance, integrity and values so much.

A nice example of a CEO doing this is Mike Roman, chairman of the board and CEO at 3M doing a LinkedIn post in September 2022 focused on being an ethical company.

> *"Being an ethical company committed to compliance means 3M innovation starts with bedrock principles: treating others with respect, following the rules and doing things the right way. It's who we are — from our first days in 1902 to today, 3Mers live and promote a culture of ethics and compliance.*
>
> *This month we celebrate our commitment to doing important work guided by a common purpose, promise and principles that make us a strong and ethical company. Across our company and around the world, 3Mers are proud of what we make and even prouder of how we make it. #Proud3Mer"*

His post was just a couple of paragraphs, but they speak volumes to illustrate that the upper leadership of 3M is making a proactive, public statement on the importance of ethics. Now that's some tone from the top.

CULTURE +
COMMUNICATION

Having a robust compliance program doesn't do much good if nobody knows about it. In fact, if it's so far under the radar that colleagues aren't aware of it, it's not really robust at all. Learn how to establish, reinforce and evangelize about your culture of integrity.

Freshen Up Your Long-Term Communications

We know that review and monitoring of our compliance program is a critical component of effectiveness. It's why companies choose to update and refresh their codes of conduct every several years. (If you haven't done this in recent times, why not? Same goes with your policies; ongoing monitoring and review of those and revisions are critical). But have you remembered to do the same with your hotline communication materials, especially your posters and infographics? Don't forget virtual ones like screensavers or backgrounds on company devices.

Over time, long-term communications tend to fade into the background and become a part of the furniture. They may be right in front of our colleagues, but they're not exactly increasing awareness if no one is paying any attention to them anymore. That's why it's a good practice to do new campaigns from time to time and put up new posters to recapture attention and prevent stagnation from creeping in.

> **Pro tip:** An interesting data analytics measure you can take is to keep an eye on the number of hotline calls you have been getting and see if there is a change after refreshing your long-standing materials about the hotline. When I worked in compliance consultancy, one of my clients saw a significant uptick in calls after simply refreshing their posters with a redesign.

Crowdsource Communications and Training Efforts Where Possible

One of the best things about meeting other people in compliance is that we are working toward the same goal of promoting a culture of integrity within our organizations, and we often have similar pain points that hold us back from achieving our goals.

Every day around the world, compliance officers are encouraging folks to speak up, they're writing policies to guide staff and prevent misconduct and training people to, say, not commit bribery. If we're not talking to each other about those things, we're probably doing a lot of reinventing the wheel.

Before creating new materials or updating your existing ones, reach out to your compliance community. Either through group memberships or your inner circle of compliance friends, ask what materials colleagues might be in a position to share that you can tweak and rebrand for your company and offer up your own creations as well.

Some organizations have a business model where they ask you to pay membership fees to be a part of this ethics community, but there's nothing stopping you from starting up your own without cost. With the ability to share remotely, you're not even geographically bound by borders and can leverage cultural expertise and knowledge in other countries. Sanitize the content where necessary and appropriate.

Many of our awareness campaigns are applicable across geographies and industries. You may also be able to pull up publicly available materials of companies where you don't have contacts and look to see what works in their compliance policies as well.

Search engines are a compliance officer's best friend. Back in 2010, it was relatively difficult to find a compliance policy on the internet. I recall doing a search for gifts, meals and entertainment policies and could find only two examples from other organizations. Today, transparency reigns supreme and a whole host of these policies are available to view, share and benchmark to help guide your own.

Being inspired by and borrowing from others is nothing to be ashamed about, nor does it detract from your own great communication efforts. Sometimes it helps to see how other people convey important information rather than simply trying to respin your own year after year.

Run an Internal Contest for the Creation of Compliance Communication Materials

Compliance officers are probably not the first professionals that come to mind when we hear the word "creativity." We have our moments, but even those of us with the freshest, most cutting-edge ideas have only so much to offer as the years go on.

Why not pose a challenge to colleagues to compete for a prize and come up with a compliance communication campaign themselves?

Where possible, be inclusive and think about a way to use every entry in your communications campaign for the rest of the year. This way you can outsource some of the creativity demands, and your colleagues have more invest-ment in the campaigns if they or a friend/team member have contributed to them.

You can steer them with a specific theme, such as promoting speak-up culture, or keep it open-ended and ask for any materials that will raise the awareness of compliance principles and concepts.

I promise you'll be blown away by the quality of the entries submitted, even in your less-densely populated business units. In fact, I've often found that the bigger your ask, the more likely you are to be blown away. I've seen colleagues submit team photos for compliance week activities where they create a slogan and decorate themselves with local-themed paraphernalia. I have been amazed at the lengths they've gone to.

Pro tip: Don't forget to consult with the communications team about any style guide requirements that need to be followed so you can set those parameters and expectations in advance. That's a lesson I learned the hard way, and I hope it will save you some grief!

Checking Your Assumptions

Regardless of culture, background or personality type, we humans hate to have full inboxes of unread emails. The overflowing inbox acts as a never-ending to-do list.

It can be easy to project these thoughts onto our colleagues and automatically think that we need to reduce compliance email communications or tailor our program in another way based on our own assumptions and preferences.

However, the smart compliance officer tests these assumptions before changing the status quo.

Sometimes it's not enough to put yourself in the shoes of someone else, because no matter how hard we try to empathize with our colleagues, we aren't them. Surveying colleagues to ask them their preferred method of receiving communications or other program preferences they have may be enlightening.

The last time I did this, by way of a question to answer on a board at a compliance week event (remember, you should always be getting something in return from compliance week activities, not just unilaterally pushing information out), the overwhelming majority of my participating colleagues indicated that they wanted to hear from the compliance department by way of email.

It may be true that they also hate having boatloads of emails to read. That doesn't mean it's not the preferred forum of communication. Both can be true at the same time.

Empathizing with our stakeholders is important, but all assumptions should be checked.

Behavioral Clock Challenge — Peer Norming and Nudges

Our behavioral boundaries in a business are often set by leadership. After all, that's why tone from the top is such a common theme in regulator expectations for an effective program.

Taking this into account, Ezekiel Ward, chief compliance officer of Yara International at the time, introduced a culture of integrity initiative where 100 key members of management were identified for a two-pronged exercise. These managers were not necessarily C-suite but carried influence and credibility within the company by virtue of their titles or charismatic personalities.

They were asked to complete brief surveys that expressly addressed culture of integrity in relation to tone-from-the-top characteristics and self-assess themselves on these points.

These self-reflected scores are handed back to compliance to analyze for patterns and trends to identify benchmarks. Ideally, questions should be limited to something they can complete in about five to seven minutes, meaning it's not a huge time investment. You can hold a few trial runs with colleagues to set out the time estimate in your instructions so the leaders know it's not going to be a heavy lift or time investment.

The second step of the process is a one-on-one meeting with the chief compliance officer to discuss the results and see the overall scores of other leaders for peer norming purposes. The CCO can then share ideas for how to improve in the areas where a leader hadn't rated themselves so well.

Additionally, this exercise provides nudges for the participants to take advantage of. If someone wasn't previously putting compliance regularly on the agenda for their team meetings, the fact it was mentioned in the self-assessment is a hint that they might like to think about initiating that idea, especially before their upcoming meeting with the CCO!

BEHAVIORAL CLOCK INITIATIVE SELF-ASSESSMENT

Print and fill this table in. (Page 1 of 2)

Rate the following "I ..." statements on a scale of 1-5 (1 = never; 5 = always)

I regularly address ethics and compliance topics in staff meetings.	1	2	3	4	5
I am a role model for proper business conduct and integrity; I inspire my direct staff to uphold the company's standards and values.	1	2	3	4	5
I maintain an "open door" that employees are comfortable using for positive, negative or sensitive issues.	1	2	3	4	5
I take prompt action upon observing or learning about potential unethical or non-compliant behaviors and issues.	1	2	3	4	5

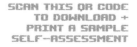 SCAN THIS QR CODE TO DOWNLOAD + PRINT A SAMPLE SELF-ASSESSMENT

Building on the Behavioral Clock Initiative

During the CCO interviews, listen for quotes from the leaders that demonstrate their commitment to ethics and integrity. Ask for permission to use the quote, and create communications using the collected nuggets, such as a poster filled with the quotes and image of the leader that ties back to their message. They'll be held account- able to the words on a long-term basis, and the poster will serve as a tone-from-the-top initiative.

Pro tip: The McDonald's supplier code of conduct is another great best-practice document that serves as an excellent example to take inspiration from when revising your own supplier-related documentation.

McDonald's has effectively deployed a similar tactic by incorporat- ing compliance-related quotes into their supplier code of conduct. The words of leaders from different regions are interspersed throughout the document. This is something that you could think about for your own code of conduct, especially if it's a digital one where updates can be made easily and in a timely manner to take into account any departures of relevant employees.

Pyramid Schemes for Sharing Knowledge Within Your Team

Legally, pyramid schemes are prohibited in most places, but when it comes to information flow, they can be an efficient structure to leverage. Make it a practice for each person in the team to report back to everyone else on the highlights and ideas they're excited about trying every time someone attends a professional development opportunity.

It's not always possible to send the whole team to the same conferences and seminars, and even when budget does allow for it, team members might choose to attend different sessions. Make sure that valuable information flows throughout the whole compliance team by way of debriefs or distributing written summaries and ideas for changes to the compliance program.

Pro tip: This can be used as part of a compendium for new joiners to the department, especially those new to compliance. To help start this resource, ask team members to suggest guidance, blogs, podcasts, news websites, book reading, thought leaders to follow and so on that can be compiled in one list and associated materials where possible, such as conference reports. The list becomes a living document that can be added to over time to create economies of scale when onboarding new staff members.

Dedication to Culture of Integrity

In 2016, Gartner (then CEB) asked compliance departments what their primary goal was; the overwhelming majority said creating a culture of integrity was their top priority. I started to conduct my own surveying and research to find out what concrete initiatives other compliance practitioners were working on to further this goal.

Surely with the majority of folks prioritizing the same thing, I'd collect scores of ideas in a short space of time. Instead of being inundated with ideas — though I did find a few gems — many peers appeared to be conflating communications activities with culture of integrity initiatives.

For example, many considered their compliance week offering to be a culture of integrity effort. In my view, compliance week is an advocacy and outreach initiative. It has the benefit of helping increase compliance awareness, providing a bit of education and polishing our brand as non-scary, approachable business enablers, to be sure.

But when was the last time a salesperson was about to embark on an imprudent deal with a naughty third party, then stopped themselves just before signing the contract and declared, "I shall not proceed with this dastardly act because I played some games during compliance week seven months ago and I have, at this moment, just been reminded about what an ethical person I am because I played those games?"

As wonderful as a compliance week is as an irregular part of your communications campaign, it lacks the repetitiveness required to help shape a culture of integrity. Without more, it's going to be difficult to effect real change.

Furthermore, when I came across counterparts who were developing and implementing workstreams that would effectively embed ethics and integrity into the DNA of the business, it was only on an ad hoc basis, something that was offered when there was time and resources but not a fundamental aspect of the compliance program.

It occurred to me that dedicating resources to promotion and measurement of a company's culture of integrity was an area of opportunity for the ethics and compliance field.

To give better proportionality to what is stated as an important goal, at a prior job, with the support of my management, I was named the head of culture of integrity and compliance education. That created the notion of a dedicated resource, along with my sterling team of the same name.

Pro tip: If your compliance function is comparatively small, you might like to consider giving someone in the compliance department responsibility for measurement of the culture of integrity program (culture of integrity survey and/or other data analytics and associated analysis) and administration of initiatives to promote your company's culture of integrity as part of a dedicated plan to promote and measure the company's culture of integrity. This will make for a more methodical and organized structuring of priorities with overt accountability, commitment and follow through.

Super-Charge Exit Interviews

It's fairly standard for many compliance officers to have negotiated some culture of integrity questions to be included in exit interviews. The trick is to make sure that the compliance department really does get passed on the information and that any ethics, integrity and compliance issues brought up under different sections of the interview are relayed to the compliance department also. What controls do you have in place to make sure you're getting the right information from exit interviews and that appropriate remedial action is occurring in a timely manner?

The co-CEOs of a compliance software company, Nick and Gio Gallo, put me on to the idea of outsourcing exit interviews so that they're conducted independently. It was a total revelation to me. Because what happens if HR is contributing to a poor culture of integrity? Employees are unlikely to give them feedback that they are the problem, and if they do, HR is not exactly incentivized to record and share with others the information that they're terrible at their job and are promoting a lack of ethics in the organization. After all, there is no second line of defense for HR.

And I'm not just picking on HR here — an independent company ensures an unquestionably objective approach with regard to any internal function.

So think about whether it makes sense to have exit interviews conducted by an objective organization to better foster trust in the process and more independence and make sure that the right departments and individuals are informed of gaps and problem areas. The independent party could be assigned to route issues based on content, triage issues that contain compliance red flags and summarize trends to the board for joint credit and remediation with HR.

Another angle in which you can think about enhancing the exit interview process is for compliance to issue its own very simple exit interview to outgoing colleagues, not with regard to substantive culture of integrity and programmatic feedback but rather with regard to the effectiveness of the function from a customer-centric standpoint. It could be as simple as issuing a text message, email or survey link with the following questions from the relevant compliance officer:

- What should I continue doing?
- What should I stop doing?
- What should I start doing?

Also consider stay interviews: By the time we get to an exit interview, yes, the colleague may feel more comfortable sharing information, but we've lost the opportunity to retain them. Think of a stay interview like a real-time, individualized employee engagement survey where the organization solicits feedback and reports back while the staff member is still employed by the organization.

Mel Stanley, a personal branding coach, also recommends using the three questions above as part of a personal branding feedback exercise to help you understand whether how you wish to come across is how you are actually being received by your stakeholders in all facets of your life.

To execute this self-awareness exercise, simply identify a number of people you know in a variety of capacities, both personal and professional, and tell them you would like their feedback and either issue the three questions above, or if you wish, ask them what words come to mind when they think of your personal brand. It does not need to be an especially formal request, but it's important not to select only your biggest cheerleaders so that you get balanced input, though definitely include some of those folks.

I've received an email from someone soliciting feedback, and when I did the exercise myself, I sent a load of text messages off to people and they responded by text message promptly in return. Not only did I find this a useful exercise, but it also has an added bonus of doing wonders for your self-esteem. You will receive a flood of positive and encouraging words that will make your day — guaranteed!

This is a recommended exercise for yourself, but you could replicate it as a group activity at an event such as a team meeting or compliance summit.

Canned Email Messaging

Similar to the concept of FAQ documents for your stakeholders, this productivity hack makes your output more scalable in terms of communicating oft-quoted information.

Create a simple document where you can type in carefully crafted email text that you find yourself expressing multiple times. It can be non-substantive, such as thanking someone for taking the time to reach out to compliance and suggesting a phone call about the issue. Or it could be an introductory paragraph explaining your role in the company for a one-off issue or to send at the beginning of a relationship with a new colleague you expect will have an ongoing relationship with you. In that case, you should include relevant details such as your time zone, additional contact details and anything else you think may be valuable to share up front.

This document is also appropriate for lengthier topics, such as explaining why the gifts, meals, entertainment and travel lodging policy exists when an internal customer asks if it is possible to give a certain gift or extend some hospitality to a third party. Followed by walking through the steps of the policy (e.g., First we consider the legitimate business purpose and intention behind giving the gift by considering the frequency of giving benefits to this third party, whether it would be customary to do so, whether or not it's cash or a cash equivalent and so on), then instructions on how to apply the relevant thresholds if the considerations are satisfied.

This idea also works well for helping newer members to the compliance department learn how to formulate written responses in a diplomatic way by sharing the precedent files between team members.

The key difference between this precedent or template document compared with FAQs is that you will still be responsible for issuing the advice and not making it available for colleagues to self-select the responses that suit them best. As much as we can expect automation to be a growing part of our lives, including in compliance departments, there is a real risk in not having the compliance experts ask the right questions to clarify the precise circumstances at hand and apply the correct, objective advice to a fact matrix presented by a colleague.

A HUMANE
COMPLIANCE FUNCTION

Both inside and outside of your compliance program, it's paramount to treat people with respect. It's not just the ethical thing to do, but it will also make your life as a compliance officer easier, as colleagues across the organization will see compliance as a partner rather than an obstacle — or worse, not think of compliance at all.

Delivering Bad News with Empathy

As genuine business partners and enablers, we take very seriously the goal of being the Department of Know rather than the Department of No. This means going to every effort to achieve the goal of the business even if we can't take the original route suggested. There are, however, rare instances where no matter how creatively we strategize, we must deliver bad news.

One of my very first jobs was advising landlords and tenants about New Zealand's residential tenancy law. The relationship between landlords and tenants can be fraught and full of emotion, and when things go wrong, very expensive for one or both of the parties.

When I was giving advice that involved applying the legal framework to each fact scenario, I was also part counselor. People were coming to me very upset and stressed in a large number of these interactions where patience and sometimes goodwill was frayed.

My role was particularly difficult because I had to convey the advice by way of telephone conversation, so it was audio only. I couldn't express my empathy and concern by way of facial expressions or body language.

I tried many approaches to best help my clients, sort of a trial-and-error process. There was one opening in starting off my response that proved to be more effective than any others. This gave my constituents a sense that I cared, and it softened the blow I was about to deliver.

That sentence was, "I know this isn't the news you were hoping to hear ..."

I have found that when people feel we are on their side and genuinely interested, they are more likely to be accepting of the bad news and move on to a path that better serves them. Penny Milner-Smyth, an organizational behavior specialist, provides some additional insights on benefits of such a phrase:

> *"It's an opening line that has application in the many situations where we are required to communicate decisions that may not be what the recipient wants to hear.*
>
> *To understand the value of Mary's approach it is important to examine the experience of the person receiving the news from a neuroscience perspective.*
>
> *Neuroscience is a multidisciplinary field, and in this instance we must draw from both affective neuroscience (the study of the neural mechanisms of emotion) and cognitive neuroscience (the study of the neural mechanisms of cognitive processes such as comprehension, reasoning and judgement).*
>
> *What we know is that neural mechanisms associated with the emotion of fear can have a profoundly disruptive impact on our ability to engage the cognitive processes we need to respond in a considered and rational way in the face of bad news.*

The situation in question means that at least two of the factors that heighten fear in the brain may be present for the recipient: uncertainty and ambiguity. In contrast, the factors that the brain craves for optimal functioning include predictability and clarity.

One of the typical mistakes we make is to preface unwelcome news with a preamble that we imagine will cushion the blow. This often includes giving a justification for the decision that is yet to be conveyed and providing assurance that a fair process has been followed (just think of a situation where we are telling someone they have been unsuccessful in applying for a promotion).

In the case of any application rejection, until the outcome is received, the person is living in a state of unpredictability — unable to have an adequate level of confidence in what the future holds.

What happens during the 'preamble approach' is that the receiver's fearfulness is increasing as the outcome is clearly imminent. The heightened sense of foreboding actually interferes with the recipient's ability to attend to and comprehend what the speaker is saying. Effectively, the delay increases the extent to which fearfulness is compromising rational thinking ability. 'Where is the preamble leading?' This ambiguity amplifies the fear already caused by the uncertainty.

It is no surprise that we find ourselves in situations where people seem to have 'not heard' what we are telling them — their capacity to make sense of our message has been compromised by our inadvertent heightening of the disruptive fear emotion.

The moment Mary conveyed the outcome, with empathy and without delay, the recipient [would] typically experience not just disappointment but the certainty that comes from knowing that a given avenue is no longer available to them. This certainty can have a calming effect that enables the recipient to shift into a rational, forward-looking mental state. Coupled with the evident empathy conveyed in Mary's opening line, the recipient feels supported — able to continue with the conversation in a state not of exacerbated fear but one of greater 'neuropsychological safety.'

We should not expect that this approach will always be met with a calm response by a disappointed recipient, but we can have confidence that we have not inadvertently exacerbated an already emotionally loaded conversation. In some instances, this brain-friendly approach will, in fact, lay the foundation for a fruitful discussion between the two parties that positions the recipient to move forward positively."

Try prefacing your substantive update with this phrase next time you have to convey an unfavorable message to colleagues, whether it be a member of the business or with someone on your team.

Optimize Your Case Intake Procedures

"You mentioned doing things blindly. I think there's so much opportunity for companies to make better use of the case intake process." This astute comment was made by Tyler Walker, a team lead at a compliance vendor.

I thought for a moment about his observation and saw pretty quickly that he was correct. Yes, we sometimes use the case intake process as an educational opportunity and a chance to reassure colleagues that we take their complaints seriously. But Tyler is right — there is so much more that we could be doing. How might you tweak the case intake process to add value to your compliance program or make the reporting process a more satisfactory one for the reporting person?

We already know that our reporting-line data is a rich source of information that can be deployed in quantitative data analytics studies. Could it be a better qualitative data opportunity as well? Let's be clear: This is not the time to deploy a culture-of-integrity survey and ask a million questions, but perhaps one or two extra, specially targeted questions in the intake process could provide a wealth of useful information that instills more trust and faith in internal processes with the current reporter and your reporters of the future.

Here is my idea: Prioritize one or two things about the current reporting process you're not satisfied with and want to improve. If you need some inspiration for an area to focus on, grab a copy of the latest hotline benchmarking reports from service providers in the space and compare your data against them. Where you are significantly behind the benchmark, circle those areas to work on as a part of this exercise. Then insert a question into your case intake process for the third-party call center operator to ask that will help you to better improve your reporting successes by understanding some of the root-cause issues specific to your organization when it comes to common obstacles and aspirations.

Area of improvement	Question for intake process
Increasing reports to internal channels	We're so grateful you took this important step to report. May I understand what made you select the compliance action line as your preferred reporting channel? OR Thank you so much for raising this concern with me today. Speaking up was the right thing to do. May I check whether you raised this issue internally before speaking with me today? If yes, what was the reaction; if no, why not?
Increase reporting rates	I know that sometimes it can take a bit of courage to call us. What persuaded you to take the step to reach out to me today? OR Is there anything that caused you hesitation before reaching out to me today that I can reassure you about?
Decrease perceptions of retaliation	[Where relevant] You've mentioned that you are scared of being retaliated against for making this report. I want to reassure you that we have a strict non-retaliation policy which I'm happy to send it to you if you would like a copy. Could you give me some more information about why you feel retaliation could happen to you? OR

SCAN THIS QR CODE
TO DOWNLOAD +
PRINT A SAMPLE
INTAKE QUESTIONS

This anonymized information can help you address perennial compliance reporting line improvement areas by targeting data mining to give you the right information to take action.

Tweak Tone From the Top by Adding Value

I like to challenge myself by thinking of a new and different way to demonstrate tone from the top in training each year.

It's a standard best practice to feature your company's CEO at the beginning of your compliance policy documents and your compliance training to help demonstrate that your program has a consistent tone from the top.

Typically, the CEO appears in training emphasizing how important compliance is and encourages colleagues to take the training module and finish it on time. The thing is, if the CEO is making the effort and commitment to appear in a compliance training in the first place, it's clear they stand behind the initiative.

Training costs an awful lot to deliver to your staff, not only in terms of the compliance department's costs, but also with respect to the fact that for every minute a colleague takes doing compliance training, the company loses a minute of productivity from their core jobs they were hired to do.

We must take this opportunity cost seriously and use every moment of our training wisely. Instead of having the CEO parrot the fact that compliance is important and they expect staff to complete the course by the deadline, let their presence speak for itself and use their appearance as an opportunity to teach about a learning objective within the training.

That's right, turn your CEO into an adjunct compliance professor. A good opportunity for this is the values section of code of conduct training. Interview your CEO on how they have seen the company's values lived out over the past year, what the values mean to them personally and so on.

Why not take this initiative a step further by incorporating some tone from above as well? Ask the head of every region to teach some content in the training. Assign them a subject and provide high-level talking points that they can turn into their own story and supply you with a video. Tone from above is even more relatable and influential for staff in large companies where many colleagues may not be familiar with the global CEO's name, let alone seen their picture before — and certainly have never met them or conversed. As the years go on, other leaders and influential or charismatic staff can be featured from various levels of the business.

You can also evolve this idea by changing the way in which the leaders are presented. For example, instead of videos, try using cartoons (flattering ones, not offensive caricatures!) of the selected leaders and a speech bubble with a quote from the leader teaching on compliance topics.

Create an Official Mentoring Program for Compliance Department Staff

Seeking out a mentor can be tough. Instead of putting the onus on your colleagues to organically find a mentor or pose the awkward question to a stranger of "Will you be my mentor?" think about establishing a formal program with mentor/mentee matching and even a policy to place some rigor around the program.

Ask your compliance program advisory board, which we talked about earlier, if there is anyone willing to be a mentor for diversity of thought from those outside of compliance, as well as your wisdom council participants (see bonus section at the end of this book) if they might like to be matched with someone from your company.

Don't forget about reverse mentoring, in which someone with perhaps less compliance experience has some other skill or expertise to offer a seasoned compliance professional. In my case, I get a lot of reverse mentoring from folks who have stronger technology prowess than me.

Not a CCO but like the sound of this? There's nothing stopping someone who is not a member of the management team from stepping up and volunteering to coordinate such an effort. You'll get a reputation for being proactive and helpful if you offer — this goes for almost any other initiative under the sun, as well. Letting your CCO know that you would like to make yourself available for initiatives that benefit the team will certainly be looked upon favorably.

Pro tip: In a similar vein, even if you haven't been tapped for an open role you're keen on in the department with higher responsibilities, don't take that as a sign that you're automatically rejected for the role. Apply anyway. Don't self-reject. Even though you may not get the job, you've clearly signaled to management that you're looking for bigger and brighter things, and they'll keep you in mind for future opportunities.

Ethics Notecards and Small Gifts

Many of us acknowledge that incentives should form part of an effective compliance program. There are some detractors who are of the view that people should be ethical simply because it's the right thing to do. While I think if we operated in an ideal world the latter view would be the case, the reality is not only that we do not live in an ideal world, but also that the Department of Justice and Securities and Exchange Commission espouse incorporating incentives into programs in the FCPA Resource Guide:

"DOJ and SEC recognize that positive incentives can also drive compliant behavior. These incentives can take many forms such as personnel evaluations and promotions, rewards for improving and developing a company's compliance program, and rewards for ethics and compliance leadership."

For those reasons, I think it makes sense to include incentives in some way in your program.

There are logistical and pragmatic considerations involved in adjusting the performance review process to incorporate incentives. For example, how do you deal with staff who are far more likely to be exposed to tough business ethics situations, such as sales personnel, as opposed to, say, an administrative assistant who likely won't have the chance to heroically turn down outrageous bribery opportunities? How do we account for that in our performance review evaluations?

(That said, and as an aside, you also can't assume that there is no improper inducement risk for colleagues in administrative assistant roles. I remember being amused many years ago by an administrative assistant at a party learning I was in compliance. She told me that she decided to move staff celebratory events to a new hotel from one where she had booked many events previously. The previous venue began sending her cakes and inviting her to special events as their guest. She knew they were trying to woo her and win back her business with improper benefits. They may not have been exorbitantly priced, but she knew as well as we do reading this, that there was corrupt intent. I do love being able to use the phrase "Low risk doesn't equal no risk!"

For any compliance officers wringing their hands still, I am pleased to inform you that our hero administrative assistant refused to partake in the improper inducement. She instructed them to stop sending her baked goods or she would return them, and she did not attend any of the events dangled temptingly in front of her. She also stuck to her guns and continued to use the vendor that she had assessed as suiting her department's needs better.)

But back to our main objective with this hack: A less convoluted way to incorporate incentives into your program can be by way of customized appreciation and small gifts.

In addition to being less of an implementation headache, this idea is budget friendly. Order a large number of greeting cards that can be sent from members of the compliance department to recognize assistance and role modeling of ethical behavior and give thanks (for example, to leaders who have arranged to provide a prize for an annual compliance week). You can get customized ones tailored specifically to your requirements. I have put text on past ones like, "I Make Time for Honesty and Integrity" to fit in with the behavioral clock theme we've talked about and had small gifts to accompany them.

I chose whiteboard magnets that were the same design as the card, and fortuitously, these seamlessly became fridge magnets when Covid-19 took hold and working from home replaced the office environment. I recommend something small and non-bulky because it makes for economical postage when getting them out to colleagues who do not reside in the same geographical area — a real consideration when overseas shipping costs apply for international teams.

Pro tip: I have leveraged this idea in my personal capacity when sending end-of-year appreciation cards to my wider team. It's a great way to support local artists. I looked on Etsy and found an artist who could visually re-create an in-joke the team enjoyed, and these were turned into fridge magnets I slipped into greeting cards that went all over the world.

In light of the pragmatic issues outlined above, in my opinion, it is a lot easier to incorporate punishments, including clawbacks, into your program to disincentivize, though, of course, we do need to aim for both. If you're struggling with a way forward to address U.S. government expectations around your company's good-faith efforts to try to recoup money from naughty executives, formalizing clawbacks as a clear and transparent consequence in your disciplinary matrix is a good way to approach it.

Compliance Office Hours

Taking into account different time zones of your colleagues, set one or two compliance office hours sessions periodically where people can drop in with any kind of question, whether it be about part of the due-diligence process or the difference between when to go to the compliance team and when to go to legal.

Make it a safe place where psychological safety reigns supreme. In promoting these sessions, let people know that you don't care if they have a question they think they are supposed to know the answer to or need help with a subject that's been covered in a training. Make it clear that all you care about is that you're able to help clarify any gray areas they have and that the goals are:

- They walk away having their questions answered or
- You've heard your colleague if they have used the meeting as an opportunity to share feedback or an idea for the compliance program.

Ozan Varol, a rocket-scientist-turned-law professor, recommends an approach to encourage questions that he learned from teaching students. Instead of asking, "Does anyone have any questions?" say something like, "The material we just covered was really confusing, I'm sure there are plenty of you with questions, now is a great time to ask them."

This creates psychological safety by normalizing confusion and questions. The same can be applied in the office to help people get over fear of embarrassment for raising something in front of their peers. When Varol flipped the script, he saw a marked increase in the number of questions he was asked, which was important because when he took the earlier approach, the test scores of his students showed that they were confused but not asking questions.

If you didn't just recently teach something, as may be the case in an office hours session, state that the compliance programs, laws, regulations and policies we have to keep on top of can be overwhelming and confusing instead to elicit the desired reaction within that context.

If your company doesn't have a very in-depth orientation program, you can encourage managers to suggest to new joiners that they join the next office hours session after arriving at the company.

Depending on the number of colleagues you have and how new your function is, the frequency of these drop-in meetings will vary. Once a month or once a quarter might be appropriate periods of frequency, perhaps ramping up to once a week for special periods when new technologies, processes or policies are implemented.

Alexis Wermuth, a compliance executive in the medical device space, likes to choose a theme topic to talk about for half of the time and then spend the rest of the time taking miscellaneous queries and comments.

Conduct Career-Mapping Sessions with Each Department Member Periodically

Some people want to keep climbing the ladder in a way that is intuitive, such as compliance intern, then analyst, then manager, then director, then vice president and, finally, chief compliance officer. Others deliberately want non-linear paths and to experience different worlds — sometimes metaphorically, though in my case, it was literally. Some don't realize that there are other options to consider than what they have in mind and are blown away to explore other possible ways to use their skill set.

I like to be up front with my team that I know there is likely a life for them after our current employer, and I'm there to support them with their wider goals.

Career mapping is about asking someone what their long-term goals are and supporting their shorter-term goals, even if the longer-term goal means you're not working together anymore. This is one of the surest ways you can let each individual on your team know that you care about them.

It's important to remember that while the team and company goals are a priority, when your employees feel like they matter, you're fulfilling one of their basic needs. This in itself is all the motivation you need to do it, but the bonus is that, according to recent research, employees who feel cared for are more likely to be engaged in their work than those who don't (94% vs. 43%), and they are more likely to stay at the company for three or more years compared to those who don't feel cared for (60% vs. 7%).

So by putting in place initiatives that show care for each employee's future and well-being, you're making it more likely that you'll hit company and team goals.

Brazenly Be Your Kooky Self

You can be professional and competent and still be unapologetically you: Those concepts do not have to be mutually exclusive. We are in a field where being human is typically seen as a positive. Let your uniqueness shine through.

Something I am very well-known for is having a Hello Kitty phone case. It gets a lot of compliments outside the workplace, but it also brings a certain freshness and personality to my work persona that helps colleagues see me as a little less strict, stuffy and boring — and a lot more human.

In other words, have the courage to bring some aspect of your whole self to work to be more relatable and approachable.

Getting the compliment, "You're pretty cool for a compliance officer" is one of the highlights of my career, especially because I'm a huge nerd!

OUT OF THE BOX

———————

Please pardon the use of a cliche, but improving the effectiveness of your ethics and compliance program sometimes means thinking differently. Not every idea here will be right for every organization, and that's OK, but remember — you don't have to do things the way they've always been done just because that's how things have worked in the past.

Be Daring, Be Different

Be inspired by something random, totally not compliance related and ask yourself how you can apply it to your program. These "outrageous" ideas are wonderful for injecting some fun into your program, which helps tremendously with ridding your function of the stale, stuffy and serious reputation. Or be inspired by a gap in your compliance program and think of a creative way to address it.

For part of compliance week one year, we had a "Flat Lisa" activity where a photo of the chief compliance officer, Lisa Estrada, was provided to staff via email and the task was to print her out, take a photo with her and caption your selfie. The impetus for such an activity was from our compliance week the year before when we did the data analytics gap analysis activity described earlier and learned that not everyone knew the name of the CCO (!). This is why it's always so critical to check on the baseline knowledge that you think people have, because there is no lowest common denominator. We need to continuously communicate critical information.

This activity idea stemmed from "Flat Stanley," a character in an American children's book series who could be mailed around the world and taken wherever you go. I never read the books myself (not a bedtime staple in New Zealand, I'm afraid), but with only the briefest of explanations, I was all in on the idea once it came up in our planning sessions.

It's nice when everyone understands a pop culture reference in compliance training, but just because an idea is inspired by something the whole audience is not privy to, that doesn't mean it's not a great idea to run with.

We also had an inflatable obstacle course as part of our carnival theme another year for colleagues to race each other. You better believe a boatload of adults jumped, climbed and dove around in their socks!

Want to show that you're cognizant of a difficult topic, but no one wants to raise it to compliance because they don't want to look like they're not on board the compliance train? Bring an inflatable or plush toy elephant with you when you enter a conversation or make a presentation and you can then use it to segue into addressing the elephant in the room. If budget is an issue or you're meeting virtually, put a picture of an elephant up as your background temporarily instead.

Now, if you're sitting here thinking, "You and your Hello Kitty phone case just won't fly at my company, Mary. It's not worth the risk of trying this in my serious and stuffy business, we're adults!" — I totally hear you. I have certainly worked for companies that aren't on the cutting edge and seem to value stoic tradition where the fun and frivolous would fall flat, or worse, not be taken seriously and risk ridicule.

Kim Yapchai used to have to deal with the same reservations. She would have an idea and others would be skeptical: "We could never do something like this at this company." But that didn't stop her from having the courage to go out on a limb and bring novelty to her company and compliance program. She expected that the compliance team could introduce something different from the usual and gain traction year on year, slowly getting the business on board. But the reception was far more positive and instant than she could have expected — the idea went viral internally.

Kim and her team ran a meme competition using the company chat as the forum. This was beneficial in that it was transparent and easy to track — not just sitting in somebody's inbox to collate and present. They picked a theme, "Integrity Always," which is one of their company values, and collaborated with a trademark lawyer to help outline the boundaries of what types of images were acceptable to use. Colleagues were invited to submit memes demonstrating the theme, and everyone was invited to vote for their favorites. The meme with the most votes won a prize.

What does this tell us? These fears are common among the compliance community: We're either experiencing them ourselves or naysayers are trying to talk us out of unusual ideas. However, the payoff of bravery, of increasing your own risk appetite, can be life-changing for how compliance is viewed by the business. There is a huge difference between being fun and novel or being inappropriate and unprofessional. We never want to be the latter, and we can share our success stories of the former to encourage others that it's OK to try innovating and leveraging pop culture.

As an aside, one of the commonalities Kim and I have discussed is that when we hold contests that involve some degree of investment of time and effort by colleagues, such as team photo contests with compliance captions in my case, choosing a topic as part of a code of conduct launch in Kim's case and inviting colleagues to create videos on the topic as a content, we are always blown away by the levels of participation and sophistication of deliverable that our colleagues come up with.

Some of the videos submitted by Kim's colleagues became official training materials. We assume that hardly anyone will want to take part or have the time to participate in our little compliance game, but the reality is that every time we have offered the opportunity for colleagues to engage with us in a creative way, they have stepped up, collaborated and impressed us. Every. Single. Time.

Everyone is busy, but we choose to make time for things that we love or fascinate us. You may not get everyone to love compliance, but you certainly can come up with initiatives that intrigue and fascinate colleagues.

Kim adds, "I think that this approach also activates your employee base so they become part of the compliance team. People aren't stupid. They generally know what is right and wrong. We just need to get them involved. … I have also found that approaching employees with something unexpected also gets them to drop their guard and listen to you."

There is something incredibly disarming and endearing about moving out of your comfort zone, away from tradition and legacy activity with outside-the-box thinking. Indeed, it does draw attention and, as Kim says, creates space for others to pay attention.

Essentially for this technique you're asking yourself, what's the last thing someone would associate with compliance — and how can I prove them wrong?

Applying Disruptive Thinking to Your Compliance Program

Disruptive thinking had its moment circa 2016, and though it's not the buzzword it once was, there is certainly value in deploying the approach to innovate and level up your compliance program. Essentially, disruptive thinking is simply thinking differently.

The clearest way this approach can be made to resonate with compliance folk is referencing that classic risk scenario of doing things the way we've always done them. Whenever we ask someone in the business why they engage in a certain practice and they respond, "Well, that's the way we've always done it," we know it's worth taking a second look as to whether that rationale is, in fact, prudent from an ethics and compliance standpoint.

Disruptive thinking challenges doing things the way we've always done them. This is important in light of new developments in your business, the evolution of the compliance field and best practices, as well as the advancement of technology.

Take a look at the conclusion of this book to get inspiration for some coaching questions you can ask yourself and colleagues to help encourage disruptive thinking and prompt new ideas to shake up your program.

Try starting with the processes and documents that you recall have been around the longest without recent monitoring and review. Don't forget ancillary elements of your compliance program, such as your key performance indicators (KPIs). Part of good monitoring and review of our programs is not just on the actual seven elements as outlined by the U.S. Sentencing Guidelines for Organizations or other guidance-dictated substantive areas but also on the wider elements that holistically comprise our compliance programs.

When it comes to KPIs, ask yourself when you last reviewed them after they were put into place. If the answer is never, take a look and ask whether they are still fit for purpose and whether they are actually measuring what you had intended to measure. Then apply some disruptive thinking questions, too.

Obtain Promotional Vendor and Company Items as Giveaways

Ask compliance vendors and your internal marketing teams if they have any low-value promotional items left over from previous campaigns they would like to donate to you for compliance week activity giveaways. This is a great way to save budget for you to spend on major prizes and touch more colleagues with compliance fairy dust!

A good opportunity for this is when a large conference is coming to your town. You can offer to take away any of the leftover giveaways on the last day of the conference so that the marketing teams don't have to worry about the hassle of carrying or shipping them back to headquarters and figuring out how they'll use the meager supplies themselves.

Pro tip: If you're a vendor reading this, note that it is a good way to have a conversation with in-house colleagues you've perhaps never spoken to before and a way to meet new people. Be very careful of insinuating that you're expecting something in return — that will put both you and the recipient in a risky situation. In order to be compliant, it must be done with a full heart and as a gesture of goodwill.

Hopefully, with this readership, it goes without saying that this is strictly a non-quid-pro-quo situation and vendors are not promised additional business if they choose to surrender their overflow, minimal cost items.

Scavenger Hunt Orientation Exercise

Set yourself apart right from the start by demonstrably showing you're not one of those "sheriff" compliance officers who is stuffy and dry. You think outside the box and can have fun.

Instead of a boring, didactic presentation about the compliance function where one poor soul repeats the same text and goes through the same slide deck during every orientation, turn the session into an activity where new colleagues need to find the organizational chart to identify elements like the chief compliance officer, their direct compliance officer, where on the intranet/internet the code of conduct and other compliance policies can be found, how to access the contact details for the reporting hotline and whatever else you need to communicate as a priority.

The medical-training adage of "see one, do one, teach one" is right up there in my book with the most effective learning techniques. This exercise allows people to trial-navigate the company resources for themselves in an environment where they are guided, so that when they need it, they'll be more likely to replicate what they already did in orientation and access valuable compliance department information when they need it in the future.

This is a scalable way to bring a breath of fresh air and distinction to the way you induct new colleagues, and it saves a live presenter from repeating the same spiel over and over. Rather, they can be a facilitator of the activity and answer questions, which is much more interesting for the compliance representative! You have probably already guessed what I'm about to say next — you can have prizes for the first person to turn in the correct responses.

Dawn Raid Just-In-Time Training

Just-in-time training is rightly lauded for being a user-friendly technique to deploy as a part of your compliance program.

It can range from the very simple, from a note on trash cans asking if health/confidential/other sensitive information has been shredded to walking colleagues step-by-step through a highly fraught situation, such as when there are unannounced visits by authorities often known as dawn raids.

As you can imagine, even the most calm and collected person is not going to be in the best position to remember every part of your dawn raid training from 14 months ago as officials stand before them demanding access to information.

So, we need to help them in this crucial moment.

I still remember how panicked I was when barred from entering a country over visa allegations, which was likely a shakedown for a facilitation payment. Even though I had trained others on it several times before and knew by heart what to do, it was still scary knowing that the balance of power wasn't entirely on my side. If experienced compliance professionals feel nervous in such high-pressure situations, how can we expect our colleagues to feel any better or be expected to recall the minutiae of our training when it's not what they repeatedly have to think about?

In these circumstances, having a one-page quick-reference document can really make a difference. To prepare your document, have an infographic of a handful of concisely written steps for the front desk staff to go through should this ever happen to your organization. For example: 1. Request officers' identification, 2. Ask to view search a warrant and so on. Print it out and keep it in a drawer at reception.

Remember that due process can vary from jurisdiction to jurisdiction in terms of what regulators have the power to do when conducting unannounced visits, so make sure your instructions are in line with local laws and requirements.

On the back side of the reference sheet, have a list of names and phone numbers of staff from legal and compliance. List several people from each department and your external law firm so that if someone is not available to answer their phone, there are plenty more options of appropriate staff and/or external counsel to get in touch with quickly.

Your Email Signature as a Changing Billboard

Where not prohibited by company policy, use your email signature block to display messages to colleagues about compliance. For years now, many compliance professionals have added cute ethics quotes or the hotline details to their email signature blocks. That's nothing terribly new.

However, Adam Balfour, who oversees the global enterprise risk program for a multinational corporation, levels up on this old idea by changing his message frequently (including a compliance tip of the month!), and having more sophisticated knowledge of Microsoft Outlook features, he is able to have a standard message for the first email received from a recipient, which is then replaced by another message when his colleagues are replying to a new message in the chain.

To do this yourself, go into the settings of Outlook messages by opening a new email. Click the "Signature" downward arrow, then option "Signatures ..." On the top right corner of the new window, you can then choose what signature message will show for new messages and what will show for replies and forwards.

Pro tip: You can also use your out-of-office message for this purpose or your personal branding and stakeholder rapport building. For example, when you're going on vacation you can talk a little bit about the destination or a celebration you're attending, reminding folks that yes, we in compliance like fun stuff and have lives, too. If you're out of the office to speak at a compliance conference, accept an award or other incredible tooting-your-own-horn moment ("blowing your own trumpet," as we say in New Zealand), share where you'll be and a little bit about your speaking topic or accolade for some gentle self-promotion.

Mystery Shop Your Compliance Program

A fairly common test compliance folks run is to try calling their independent reporting hotline number to check on the level of service they receive to understand what colleagues go through when making a compliance report. Ideally you'll want to understand how long it took before the call was answered (we don't want people to be deterred and give up when they're already on the fence about reporting as it is), whether the liaison can answer basic compliance questions, whether they can promptly provide someone when requested who is fluent in the promised languages, whether they ask good questions to elicit information from the reporter, whether they are courteous, respectful, empathetic and so on.

This technique can be applied by putting yourself in the shoes of your internal clients and the colleagues using your compliance program.

To take your monitoring and review initiatives further, ask a couple of colleagues in different areas of the business to help you by issuing a question to their compliance officer and the compliance training specialist or to send you the last interaction they had with your department via email and review the responses they get in return.

- What is the responsiveness of the compliance team?
- Are the answers helpful and to the point?
- Are they in plain language and not legalese?
- Are they customer-centric?

Ask to be enrolled in training programs for sales or other staff that you would not ordinarily be issued.

- Is the training material patronizing or too easy to be useful?
- Are relevant scenarios and examples provided?
- Do you feel it was a good use of your time to attend the training?
- Did you encounter frustrating technical issues with the learning management system?

Sit in on a live compliance training or presentation.

- Are good presentation skills deployed?
- Does the presenter speak clearly and use good examples?
- How did the presenter's demeanor add to the perception and reputation of the compliance program?
- Was the session an appropriate length?
- How were questions handled? Were questions invited?
- Looking around the room, how attentive were the learners?

65 HACKS + CHEAT CODES TO LEVEL UP YOUR ETHICS + COMPLIANCE PROGRAM
PROGRAM MYSTERY SHOPPING SAMPLE QUESTIONS
(Page 1 of 2)

Sit in on a presentation or training session you wouldn't normally attend, ideally at the back of the room.

1. How does the presenter/facilitator command the room and audience?

2. Where are attendees directing their attention at the beginning of the presentation, at the midway point and nearing the end of the scheduled time?

3. Is information presented in various ways or only through a lecture?

4. How does the facilitator handle questions?

5. Was it difficult to sit through?

SCAN THIS QR CODE
TO DOWNLOAD +
PRINT A SAMPLE
MYSTERY SHOPPING
AUDIT

Critically read the compliance policies with fresh eyes or select one of the key sections and ask a colleague to candidly tell you whether the section makes sense to them and how would they explain what it means in their own words. State that you're not there to judge or report back to anyone such as their boss, you simply genuinely want to know if you're adequately serving colleagues. Advise that if the policy is not clearly stated, that's on compliance to fix and not the fault of the participants.

Another angle for mystery shopping is checking in on the core business knowledge of your compliance team members to make sure that they are going to efforts to absorb who does what in the business, what the business lines are, key products and services, as well as the full gamut of business lines. Louis Sapirman, a veteran chief compliance officer, notes that "Compliance is rarely done well sitting behind a desk." It's necessary to get out there, meet people and learn about the business.

I remember fondly back to an afternoon in Singapore over a decade ago where my peer, Karina Vollmer, and I were sitting in front of the general counsel, John Freeman, in his office. He started rattling off a list of business segments of the international telecommunications company that we worked for and we had to answer the rapid-fire departments with the name of which colleague led which segment. Though John's style is not to intimidate (he's the one that modeled a learning moment for me as an internal investigation interview newbie that I could be effective in bright and breezy interactions and not only in "You can't handle the truth" desk-thumping moments. Thanks, John!) it was a good, quick session in which we learned we needed to put name to the team and better understand our business.

Play a Little Game of 'The Price is Right'

The old-school approach to compliance education has often been scaring colleagues stiff with stories of astronomical pecuniary penalties paid by naughty companies and horror stories about individuals receiving prison terms. Things have changed since then.

We know that's not especially effective, and it most certainly it doesn't help our reputation in compliance to provide education in such a manner. However, it is possible to incorporate awareness of penalties in a more lighthearted way. Consider playing a version of *The Price Is Right* focused on anticorruption, sanctions, antitrust, data privacy or other regulatory topics using the relevant fines each company received as the "prices."

There's a QR Code for That

One of the lingering practices from the pandemic has been the encouragement of restaurants to continue providing access to their menus by way of scanning a QR code with our mobile phones. It is possible this practice will be here to stay.

Use of QR codes was not quite so ubiquitous in "the before times," however, they were sometimes used as tools in programs previously.

The first time I saw a QR code deployed in a program, it was back in 2014. A luxury automobile maker I visited had a reporting helpline poster with QR code at the bottom right-hand corner for colleagues to access further information about speaking up and the reporting process. This allowed the poster to have crisp text and concise messaging while providing quick, easy, accessible details for anyone who needed them.

Pro tip: There are plenty of QR code generators available at no cost which you can find by doing a quick search on the internet.

A company in the oil and gas space has a QR code that takes colleagues straight to the company's code of conduct. They make good use of the QR code to promote the code widely and even have it included in their email signature block of compliance staff for an omnipresent reminder and ease of reference.

At a previous workplace, my colleagues used QR codes to great effect in workspaces where team members did not necessarily have their own email address or computer/ laptop but still needed to access company information or learning management system electronically. We were able to have colleagues scan a QR code that takes them straight to compliance training, which could be completed on their mobile phone.

Incentivize Action With Non-Monetary Prizes

One of my favorite creative ideas comes from two of my former team members, Jasper Quak and Mira Eigler. You know the age-old advice of asking someone lots of questions about themselves to be an interesting conversationalist? This idea leverages the natural self-interest humans have in a way that also takes the spirit of compliance champions to new levels. They came up with the concept of offering an avatar or character of a colleague within a compliance training as a reward or prize.

In addition to being something novel, unique and directly related to compliance, there are logistical benefits to offering such an incentive instead of more traditional incentives. First of all, there's no messy administrative need to cross-charge the cost of a prize across borders when choosing something that will broadly appeal to any demographic and making sure it gets to the recipient. The delivery of this prize remains within the control of the compliance department to get the artistic rendering created, making the individual a compliance hero for all in the company to see.

The implementation is pretty simple, too. When creating your next compliance training that will have a broad audience, draft a scenario where you have a character created with artistic rendering closely resembling the winner of the prize — you'll likely need to ask them to email you a photo of themselves, name the character after them and ensure that their role in the scenario is one that has an entirely positive light.

Pro tip: Hold regular catch-ups with your communications department to identify synergies and overlap.

There's no end to the initiatives for which you can offer this prize, but as it's something so different from traditional prizes and incentives, it is best saved for an opportunity where you really need to get the attention and participation of colleagues. You'll be able to keep it a coveted prize by offering it sparingly.

Consider using this method as a special way to combat survey fatigue in those times when you need to, say, issue a culture of integrity survey around the same time other departments are issuing their own surveys by entering everyone who completes the survey in a drawing to win the prize.

Gamify Your e-Learning Opportunities

Candidly, this idea isn't going to directly increase the effectiveness of your compliance program. It will just provoke the interest and attention of your colleagues in a different way — not a bad thing, I'm sure you'll agree.

A couple of specific examples to do this are to take the concept of an escape-room game and create an interactive vignette, ideally one related to your core business (drawing on my past experience, let's say the scene is of a dialysis clinic), and turn certain objects (potted plants, laptop, painting on wall, etc.) into clickable "clues," which are actually just your questions on the topic you've just trained on, specifically related to the most important learning objectives of the course. Each successfully answered clue results in a key. Once the learner has earned the desired number of keys, they can escape the room — or, for our purposes, complete the training.

Another example is to design a roadmap with certain "stops" along the way, giving the learner the task of driving a vehicle to the end of the course. Using the earlier dialysis example, it might be the delivery trucks of consumables to patients for home dialysis and the idea is to complete your batch of deliveries. Each stop is complete once a question is correctly answered.

If you can't think of a way to tie these examples to your business, that's OK, choose whatever inspiration you like to transport your colleagues to a new world, perhaps something in pop culture that is topical at the time of drafting and journey through the imagination with compliance.

What's your department all about,
beyond checking boxes? Do you even
know? If you don't have a compelling
story to tell yourself, it'll be almost
impossible to inspire and engage
people throughout your organization
in a way that motivates them to
understand the role they play in
creating an ethical organization.

Draft a Mission Statement for your Department

Start as you mean to go on.

One of my responsibilities of the past was assigned to me by innovative thinker Lisa Estrada, who tasked me with running an internal marketing team from within the compliance department.

One of the first requests Lisa made of me and the team was to come up with a mission statement for our regional compliance department of around 35 staff. The mission statement would then guide our department branding moving forward as a foundational, aligned understanding of our goals.

At first, I viewed this task as something fairly simple and easy to get on with. I understood the purpose of what we were doing, but it was only as we journeyed through the iterative process of carefully crafting every sentence and mindfully selecting just the right word to convey our intentions that I began to see real value in what at first blush seemed like a basic ask.

With this idea I want to share with you:

- How we went about creating our mission statement
- The benefits and uses we found along the way

Inclusive Process

The marketing team of our compliance department was a subset of the wider team. Therefore, we wanted to ensure that, while there would be a focal group responsible for the execution of this deliverable, the whole department felt truly part of the process and that it holistically reflected our perspectives.

To gather input, we ran a session during one of our all-hands department meetings using a word cloud tool to ask everyone to vote on certain topics that we considered would inform the drafting process. This involved asking questions like "What word do you want colleagues to think of when they think of the compliance team?" Our highest-voted word in response to this question was "partner." So, we took these nuggets as valuable starting points to craft the statement, involving our colleagues across the department right from the start.

The Iterative Drafting Process

The marketing team then convened, armed with colleague input, and put draft sentences on the whiteboard. We read out loud, we erased, we debated meanings of words, perceptions and possible connotations with various interpretations of our sentences.

We asked ourselves: What is it that made us choose this profession? What is it that makes us get up in the morning? How do we see ourselves in relation to the classic reputation of a compliance department? What are we trying to achieve at our current stage of program maturity?

It was a hugely iterative process that required several sessions of meetings to align our thoughts and, perhaps for the first time, to share as a group what being in compliance meant to us. The passage we eventually came up with was simple and concise. It shows the heart, effort and care that the marketing team members took to get it just right.

When we were satisfied with what we came up with, we disseminated the draft to the full department, asking for feedback. One word was tweaked, and at last, we had our final product.

The Fruits of Our Labor

At this point, you're probably wondering what this master-piece looks like. I'm very pleased to share the final version as follows, because it's a team effort I remain proud of:

"The Ethics and Compliance Department serves as an informed business partner, helping to guide [the company] on appropriate paths to success. We assist in identifying and measuring potential areas of risk and monitoring to support compliance. While honesty and integrity are everyone's responsibility, we are here to help the business navigate through complexities and provide timely education, advice and solutions."

Applying Your Mission Statement

Before even thinking about ways in which we might communicate the mission statement, I felt the process of coming up with the statement was beneficial in itself. It was a great initial team-bonding activity for the marketing team, and through it, the department achieved a common understanding as to the direction in which we were jointly heading.

If you find yourself in a new role heading up a compliance department, I wholly recommend this as an early team-building activity. It's also appropriate for existing teams to form consensus as a group activity during your compliance retreat or other type of all-hands meeting.

We discussed adding the mission statement to the signature block of our email addresses as a way to help shape our reputation with the business, using the statement as a simple way to explain the role of the department in orientation materials for new staff, designing it and hanging in our workspaces to remind us of our greater goal and providing it to staff new to the department to bring them in on our shared values and goals.

The latter I consider especially important. Obviously, it's helpful from a practical standpoint if we're all working toward the same objectives. However, if you review the questions in most employee engagement and satisfaction surveys, there is almost guaranteed to be a question along the lines of whether the staff member understands how their role contributes to overall company objectives. Having a mission statement is an easy and clear way to help foster the understanding within your compliance department of how your puzzle piece works to serve the other functions and, therefore, the company's main goals.

Even several years later, there were times when working on various work streams that I recalled the mission statement and considered it appropriate to include it, so I sent it around to stakeholders or insert it within the document accordingly. In that sense, it remains a versatile and ever-useful piece of text. It's appropriate and helpful to share at new-joiner orientation sessions, both within the compliance department and within the wider company to help with alignment internally and across departments.

Bring in Peers as Guest Speakers

There are a lot of headline, keynote-quality, compliance-famous people out there who are very compelling speakers and have fascinating stories to tell. But sometimes the speaker fee can be prohibitive for those without large budgets.

A way to mix things up for colleagues can be asking a friend in compliance from another company to come in and talk about a selected topic. Kevin Withane, a legal and compliance expert who is working to create a positive change in the diversity, equity and inclusion space, has held a regular series of these sessions to engage his leadership team in a different way and diversify the voices singing from the compliance song sheet. It's a refreshing way to introduce novelty to the compliance program just by featuring a different face — and many folks in compliance are more than willing to lend a hand to someone in their shoes.

Sending the elevator back down is a valuable activity for many in the field!

We all have different ways of bringing messages to life. I like to refer to the law of diminishing returns and consuming donuts to get the point across: Just because you can doesn't mean you should. My friend Samantha Kelen, a CCO in the healthcare space, uses the movie *Jurassic Park* to illustrate the same point. (I'll grant that Samantha's example is snappier than mine.)

A great opportunity for getting your contacts in to speak is your annual compliance week event or your own department retreat to share ideas and get motivated by the success stories from another program. But you need not wait for a big annual event to come around; offering these sessions on a regular basis to colleagues as snack-and-learn sessions, as Kevin has done, is a fantastic initiative for your communications plan.

Something to note is that you need not keep to substantive compliance topics to leverage this idea. In the past, one of the members of my team flagged to me an interest in a snack-and-learn session on the topic of networking. While we had leaned on internal resources for many of our sessions, when I heard there was an appetite for networking, I immediately thought of an outside subject matter expert, Jay Rosen, a VP at a monitoring company who is known as the greatest connector in compliance. Jay promptly and graciously agreed to help us with this topic. After Donna Schneider gave the "Great Women in Compliance" podcast some tips on crucial conversations, she enthusiastically agreed to give a presentation on the topic to my internal department to navigate difficult conversations and communicate more effectively in the workplace.

Compliance professionals often have really interesting skills and knowledge in different areas that make for a lot of more broadly untapped potential. Lean on your networking skills to learn more about your peers and you'll have a whole host of facilitators on hand.

Be a Journalist

Two of the people I most love to ruminate with on compliance issues and best practices are journalists by training — Kirsten Liston and Matt Kelly.

Take a page out of their book: To get the most out of compliance conferences, webinars and other educational opportunities such as podcasts, imagine you've been tasked with reporting to a compliance media outlet on the panels or sessions by way of submitting an article after the event.

You'll find yourself paying attention and taking notes in a totally different way, resulting in better absorption and triggering your critical thinking of the discussions. It makes for a less passive, more focused and, dare I say it, intellectual experience. Consider not just what the speakers are saying but how what they have advised triggers an action point for your compliance department and list those.

One such gem from Jonathan Armstrong, privacy lawyer, that the audience of a webinar has received was the commentary that a lot of organizations started recording multitudes of virtual meetings during the course of the pandemic, and while staff might not have the fortitude and willingness to review them all, regulators certainly do. An action point for the audience to take back to their compliance departments: Review stored video recordings of meetings with data retention requirements in mind. Immediately purge recordings that should not be retained by the business.

Pro tip: You can actually go through with drafting the article and submit it for publication to an outlet like Corporate Compliance Insights, which could result in your increased exposure and a nice feather in your cap for your LinkedIn profile, sharing on social media feeds and addition to your resume or curriculum vitae. At the very least you'll be able to circulate your clearly written notes to colleagues who weren't able to attend and cascade knowledge-sharing throughout your department, as well as receive kudos for being so proactive and helpful — not a bad point to be able to make in your performance review with documentary evidence!

Get Ethics and Compliance Candidates Banging Your Door Down With Your Promises to Care

The compliance market varies in competitiveness depending on the maturity of the discipline in geographical regions, and perhaps the time period of the Great Resignation has been one of the toughest times for employers universally in the history of the field.

To differentiate your ethics and compliance roles on social media, be boastful about the positive type of culture and working environment you can offer, including professional development opportunities and mentoring support. Issuing communications to employees is not the only time to show our human side: Enticing team members is another prime opportunity to lose the old-school side of "professionalism," where that means only stuffy and formal, and show your true colors while putting your best foot forward.

So, if you're sharing your company's posting on LinkedIn, don't just throw the advertisement up as a post for your network without commentary. First, the LinkedIn algorithm de-prioritizes shares of another user's post, so at a bare minimum, share a link to the job posting on your company website and create a new post.

But go further than simply slapping up a post. Talk about the positives of working on your team and what can be offered to the successful candidate once in the role, especially an amazing culture of growth opportunities and psychological safety. If you're able to highlight specifics about how the team's work contributes to the company's mission and values, even better. Essentially, you're aiming to show the most human and satisfying aspects of being a member of this tribe beyond the compensation package.

For a medium-level role, this might look like this: "We take the time and effort you invest in us seriously. Your happiness, engagement and satisfaction in your job significantly impact your life beyond the workplace. For that reason, you will be included in meetings where important decisions are made, and your views will be sought frequently. We encourage a culture of psychological safety where everyone's contribution is valued, no matter what ultimate action or path we take. You play an important part in shaping the direction of the department and our projects."

For a junior role, it might look like this: "There is, for sure, a lot of work we need to get through — we're a busy and productive team. But we also know we have a responsibility to grow and develop our talent. Each team member in compliance is matched with a department mentor who will meet with you fortnightly (that's once every two weeks, Team USA) to focus on your development. We also provide monthly snack-and-learn sessions, which are substantive and technical tutorials canvassing the latest compliance cases, multi-jurisdictional regulator guidance and best practices so that you'll be able to upskill not only while gaining on-the-job experience, but also while learning about the theory behind why we do what we do."

Most importantly, avoid making promises of something positive happening in the future that you do not have sufficient control over, such as hiring more team members, increasing salary, bigger bonus, better job title and so on. Your commitments have to be genuine and sure to materialize if you communicate them.

There is nothing that gives an employee a feeling of being misled more than undertakings that are withdrawn once they have given up their status quo and been secured into your organization. Only market opportunities and offerings you can and are prepared to give in order to incentivize interest. Unless you know for sure the economy, business strategy or opinions of others (especially your superiors) will not impact your promises, don't make them.

Of all departments hiring, we have a responsibility to be unquestionably ethical and honest in our hiring practices.

Build Your Influence Outside In

Over the past several years, I have greatly increased my exposure within the field of compliance. Initially, this wasn't intentional.

It started out because I attended conferences locally in Singapore, Hong Kong and then Dubai for years and eventually wondered about whether I might be able to be a speaker at such events myself someday.

Then that day came where I got my foot in the door because Stanley Lui, who is a legend in compliance in Asia Pacific, kindly sent the elevator back down to me and recommended me as a co-panelist at a conference he was speaking at. After that, I said yes to more speaking opportunities.

Then I thought about whether I could offer some value to the compliance community by writing articles.

So I tried doing that, despite knowing I'm not a terribly strong writer, and there was positive reception by media outlets. Not self-rejecting and being vulnerable enough to throw myself at the mercy of arbiters who are experts in their field is one of the things I am most proud of. It worked out for me beautifully. If it hadn't, what would I have lost? Certainly not pride for doing something scary. At least I could say I tried and there would be no regrets.

Then Lisa Fine and I thought about doing a podcast together, so we created our own platform.

I participated in volunteer activities like Compliance Career Connection, sitting on advisory boards, agreeing to interviews, helping to plan conferences and so on.

Amid that busyness, I was posting about these activities on LinkedIn to promote them so that my network could participate or take advantage of knowledge-sharing opportunities. Sometimes I'd even post on Facebook so that my personal network could see what I was up to.

Along the way I made more concerted efforts to post regularly. We know that consistent content creation is what helps folks gain supportive followings on LinkedIn.

An unintended positive consequence of these personal branding and sending-the-elevator-back-down efforts was that my colleagues internally began to take notice — business stakeholders wanted me to present to their business units and commented on the activities I participated in outside of the company. One internal unit leader, after listening to some episodes of the podcast, asked me to lead a session for his management team. We were not connected on social media before I received this request.

I have realized that it has been helpful for my internal influence within the primary organization that employs me for my internal clients to see me as someone with influence and subject-matter expertise outside of the company and within the compliance field.

So, add your colleagues to your network on LinkedIn and the social media pages you belong to. Make a conscious effort to create posts, share ideas, comment on the ideas of others, volunteer for projects, gain exposure and build your personal brand, which not only is great for your career and resume/CV generally but also for influence at the job you're in now.

If you're feeling intimidated by this, that's understandable. This is probably the idea in this book that takes the most long-term commitment. This process typically takes years. So start slowly. Make small goals and set realistic timeframes for achieving them.

Like all the other ideas in the book, this one can be actioned immediately, but unlike many others in the book, it can't be realized immediately. Do not be discouraged if you don't build a huge LinkedIn following after a few smart posts; that's normal. You might go viral immediately, but more likely, you will slowly and consistently build a following. If you keep at it, your efforts will pay off.

Luckily, many of the goals along the way will give you boosts of satisfaction as you progress to help you keep your eye on the overarching prize: the pride in having an article published, the compliments about your speaking session and so on. Be OK with having longer-term projects cooking.

Externally Share What You're Doing in Your Compliance Program

The compliance function at the Home Depot shares posts on LinkedIn that describe the team's monthly communications campaigns on compliance topics. Mia Reini, a compliance leader at Home Depot, has explained that it's even one of her official goals to make sure there is a public-facing angle to their compliance communications.

This activity has several benefits that touch on other ideas in this book. It's excellent fodder for your personal branding and subject matter expertise-building to the wider compliance community as well as your internal stakeholders. It's sending the elevator back down to colleagues to help provide ideas and inspiration for initiatives in their programs. It allows for other subject matter experts to comment and provide suggestions to improve upon or leverage further on your initial ideas so you can continuously improve your program with complimentary outside consulting!

Improve Presentation Skills and Confidence of Your Compliance Function by Practicing Elevator Pitches

Statistically, it's unlikely these days that most of us will be lifers at our current employers. The days where many aspire to spend 20-plus years hunkered down with the same organization are long gone. I, for one, am grateful for having had the chance to experience different environments and workplaces over the course of my career — what a time to be alive!

I am also open about this with the teams that I am charged with managing and encourage them to think of me as someone they can talk to as a career coach more broadly.

With this mindset, an elevator pitch discussion can be held with your team, keeping in mind that one day they may use their elevator pitch to apply for a job externally. That's totally OK. They may also need it for applying for a role internally, to speak at a compliance conference, as a guest on a podcast, presenting a webinar, training or representing compliance at a sales kickoff.

There are endless interactions where we need to be able to appear in front of others and make a good impression. It is, therefore, unfortunate that a fear of public speaking is so common across the world. As with anything else, though practice may not make perfect, it certainly makes for improvement and less fear.

There's no single way to hold an elevator pitch practice session, but what I found worked well when volunteering with Compliance Career Connection, a group established during the pandemic to provide support to job seekers during a tough market, was to take the following steps:

- Explain the purpose of the activity
- Set clear ground rules
- Hold a round of practice
- Invite participants to provide loving feedback
- Hold a second round of practice, incorporating feedback
- Give a second round of feedback

This dual-purpose exercise helps improve public speaking and presentation skills while teaching colleagues how to put their best foot forward when introducing yourself as a self-promotion skill. The ground rules are basic: Participate as much as you can by helping others and give feedback compassionately. The precise wording I use is that we give each other feedback with love. This is to set the scene that psychological safety is the environment required to thrive when so many people feel vulnerable trying out their elevator pitch without practice in front of a group.

Some elements of a great elevator pitch to help colleagues focus their draft are as follows:

- Thirty to sixty seconds in length
- Grabs attention, ideally not conventional, formulaic, stuffy or dry (e.g. "My name is Mary Shirley, I am a compliance officer at Living Your Best Compliance Life company" — avoid this)
- Makes people want to know more
- Includes your unique selling point
- Quantifies where possible with facts and figures
- Shows your personality and outside-of-work passions
- Includes an ask if you have one
- Concludes clearly and neatly; incorporating your ask is a great note to end on (e.g., "I'm going to be around after this presentation to chat with you one-on-one about the compliance program, please join me to share your feedback or just have a coffee." External asks may be along the lines of, "I'm currently targeting a compliance director role in New York. Please keep me in mind if you hear of anything suitable at your company or within your network.")

After sharing the elements (feel free to edit my suggestions to your preferences), have each attendee practice their elevator pitch and solicit the compassionate feedback from the rest of the group, including suggestions to consider for improvement. This tailored feedback, in addition to the considerations you share, is but part of the learning process.

A significant — if not the most valuable source of development for the group — is hearing others present their elevator pitch, reflecting on what worked effectively and how they can take a similar approach and the realization that there is a huge difference between a mediocre introduction and one that really grabs attention.

Ideally, you want everyone to be able to say their elevator pitch at least twice, the initial crack at it and then the tweaked version, taking into account personalized feedback and observations from everyone else's practice. Ensure the session is long enough to accommodate multiple rounds, or schedule a second session with space in between the two for more thought and work to go into perfecting the introduction.

Emphasize that some practice will be required so that it flows off the tongue smoothly, and suggest that they might like to consider having a "wardrobe" of slightly different elevator pitches for different situations and audiences. For example, meeting someone at a networking event, an external job interview and guest on a podcast all require different angles.

Due to the vulnerability, teamwork supporting each other and potential to learn something new about colleagues during this exercise, you may wish to consider including it as an agenda item at your next department meeting or internal compliance summit.

Content checklist

- [ ] *A non-conventional approach or opener*
- [ ] *Packing a punch in a very short space of time*
- [ ] *Quantitative data or impressive facts*
- [ ] *Value proposition & unique selling factor (how you solve the other person's problem and what sets you apart from other compliance professionals)*
- [ ] *Versions for different audiences (prospective employer vs. introduction at a conference)*
- [ ] *If applicable, a call to action you want to make (example: "Please keep me in mind if you hear of any chief compliance officer roles in Chicago.")*

Round 1 loving feedback | **Round 2 loving feedback**

SCAN THIS QR CODE
TO DOWNLOAD +
PRINT AN ELEVATOR
PITCH WORKSHEET

Boost Interactivity and Understanding of Best Practices With Scenarios

Another great idea from my former team member Jasper has been to take a real-world ethics disaster and advise the audience of the basic facts, and then based on the situation, say something along the lines of "Imagine you are members of the board of this company. What do you think are the next steps you should take?" You can then have the audience make best-practice suggestions, and then drop the bomb of what actually happened in the real-life scenario so that your captive audience can marvel about how poor judgment in ethics can lead to lack of trust by relevant stakeholders and damaged reputation.

Consider asking colleagues and friends in other countries for public ethics scandal examples so the audience is less likely to know what happened to maintain the shock factor.

If current affairs are at a standstill when you need some examples, you can also consider using the DOJ opinion procedure releases. Set out the fact scenario and then ask the audience how they think the U.S. government might have analyzed the situation. Though there is less shock factor involved, some of the scenarios put to the DOJ are downright entertaining in and of themselves! You can find a list of on the Department of Justice's website.

If you're unfamiliar with opinion procedure releases, they're worth learning about as part of your program guidance arsenal. They allow for requests to be made to the DOJ about whether certain conduct would breach the Foreign Corrupt Practices Act (FCPA). Either domestic issuer companies or individuals are permitted to make a request, and the procedure should not be used for posing hypothetical queries.

It should be noted that these releases do not set precedent, but they are indicative of how the DOJ would approach certain issues, and to that extent, they provide useful considerations to allow you to set certain guidelines and parameters within your own program.

Seeking Storytelling Inspiration From Tried-and-True Stories

I'll be the first to admit that growing up, I lived a pretty sheltered life. I grew up in Tawa, a small suburb of less than 10,000 people about 15 minutes outside of Wellington City in New Zealand. My parents were very hard workers. I often get asked how I manage to do so much. The example my parents set is the answer to that.

I was painfully shy and an intense introvert with a few close circles of friends, and by and large, we all grew up in and were based in the same area. So it is probably not surprising to you that before I became an international citizen, I didn't have a whole lot of riveting stories to share.

My life was comfortable, relatively undramatic and extremely predictable. This, of course, had marvelous benefits, and for a very long time I was content with the thought of living out all my days in that same way. And that would have been perfectly wonderful, having friends around for homemade scones with cream and jam, then later a dinner party for others with a full-on roast and freshly baked cake followed by some board games.

But it didn't put me in good stead as a youngster in the workforce to tell compelling and relatable stories, except for those times when Monopoly got very intense.

As time has gone on, I've gained some pretty good stories. I traveled to Cairo during the revolution, partied in Lan Kwai Fong, conducted compliance training in four Latin American countries for sales consultants within five days, celebrated my thirtieth birthday at the Burj Al Arab, cuddled elephants in Chiang Mai, been detained in Cameroon …

But I can only really get away with telling the same story to an audience once. So even though I'm not as sheltered and inexperienced now as I was before, I still need constant inspiration for stories because I find the same audiences in front of me a lot of the time. A tactic Kevin Withane uses that suits newbies and old hands alike is to reference Aesop's Fables to tell compliance stories.

Sharing with management that they're like the boy who cried wolf when they say they have zero tolerance but don't take disciplinary action in situations brings home compliance messages in a way that people can understand across cultures. Old proverbs and sayings can be used in the same way to keep your stories fresh but familiar and relatable as well as provide you with a starting point while you're still making history in your own fabulous life.

TRAINING

This may well be the aspect of your job you spend the most time on and expend the most brainpower thinking about. But let's face it: Conducting standard compliance trainings at regular or odd intervals simply isn't enough to do the job.

Role-Play Training of Ethical Decision-Making

Think about an issue you'd like to train on. Instead of didactic content, assign colleagues characters in a role-playing scene and have them work through the scenario with other colleagues watching and able to supply advice or opinions at given times.

An example of this might be taking a sales colleague who travels through an area where your staff are repeatedly asked for facilitation payments at the border. They are told they cannot enter the country unless they pay (an unofficial) fee of $100.

Have the salesperson react in real time, let them know they can phone their boss and guide them through the experience if they get stuck. You can also throw a wrench in the works and claim the boss doesn't pick up the phone and ask them what they want to do next to simulate real-life twists and turns and keep things interesting for the group. Of course, you are sitting there as a facilitator also. Who will think to call the compliance department? Will they think to consult compliance policies? This can be played out in a virtual environment as well as in person.

The key to success for this exercise is making sure there is an environment of psychological safety and no repercussions, including peer humiliation, for making poor choices. That's why we practice, so when the time comes when poor choices matter, they know what to do!

I like to open presentations by saying that you can ask whatever you like, even if it's something you think you should already know or have been trained on before. I only care that anything you're unsure about gets clarified during this session. This can be used before the role-playing exercise also to boost the confidence of attendees so that they can feel free not to know the answer and that it's not a point of embarrassment.

Bring Transparency to Your Investigation Process

I am inspired by the Hyatt Hotels code of conduct, which notes the company's investigation process within the code itself, removing the shroud of mystery and secrecy we typically associate with investigations.

Pro tip: The Hyatt Hotels code of conduct is one of my favorite best-practice documents for a code of conduct. If you're planning to review and revise yours in the near future, I would recommend taking a look at this one for the asset- and values-based approach as well as the user-friendly language.

This document led me to create a communication campaign around transparency of the investigation process in the hope of addressing the two most common deterrents to speaking up: fear of retaliation and belief that nothing will be done about it if a concern is raised.

It is a two-pronged initiative. First of all, an interview is held in front of an audience with the head of investigations as the interviewee, and for salacious appeal, title it something like, "Investigations: Behind the Scenes." Questions are pitched to the interviewee by another compliance colleague, such as, "So what really happens during an investigation?" ,"How do you ensure that someone who reports anonymously stays anonymous?" and "What happens if a report is made maliciously as a vehicle to attack a colleague the reporter does not like?"

This was to indirectly state that if you make a report, there is a dedicated, expert and independent resource ready and waiting to receive and investigate reports thoroughly. If your organization does not share the outcome of investigations with reporters, this is also an apt opportunity to set expectations in this regard with a question like, "Do reporters get status updates and information about the outcome and disciplinary action in an investigation?"

The second prong involves a didactic session to train managers about how to receive reports, including focus on what can constitute retaliation. But everyone in the business, not just managers, was invited to attend. Why was that?

First of all, many of our independent contributors are the managers of tomorrow, and it's never too early to start educating on managerial responsibility.

Secondly, it was important for all staff to see managers being held accountable to the non-retaliation principle and have some reassurance that we're walking the walk as well as talking the talk.

Thirdly, it's not just managers who can dole out retaliation. Being ignored or excluded by peers can be a particularly painful form of retaliation. It's important for everyone to know, not just managers, that they should not do anything constituting retaliation. Finally, it's another opportunity for all colleagues to be educated on how to identify retaliation in case they ever need to report it happening to them.

Each session is followed up by a summary infographic of content including a just-in-time training aid for managers that specifically outlines the steps to take. Should they not remember all of the content from the training (and let's be honest, who can?), the next time they receive a report, they have a quick one-page reference guide to walk them through the process.

Potential steps could look like this:

- Take the report seriously. It takes a lot of courage to come forward. Acknowledge that if appropriate.
- Thank the colleague sincerely for providing the information — it is a gift. Avoid making judgment about the merit of the allegation. It is entirely possible for a disgruntled employee to be in possession of critical information.
- Ask for as much information as you can, including checking whether there might be any supporting documentation to provide.
- Assure the reporter that you will be acting immediately by informing the investigations department, which will conduct an expert and impartial investigation — or HR if a personal grievance.
- Ask the reporter if they would like to remain anonymous, and honor their wishes.
- Provide the information to the investigations department — do not investigate yourself.
- Remember to treat the reporter as you normally would and keep the matter confidential.

This list, adapted to your company's process, can easily be turned into a checklist or infographic for the quick reference sheet.

Investigation Handbook Beyond Compliance

Should colleagues in human resources not have as much investigation experience as you, it can be helpful to offer to create a short manual for them to help with consistency in investigatory approaches across the organization.

In my experience, HR will not necessarily solicit this type of support, but if it is offered, they are incredibly gracious and grateful, acknowledging compliance as investigation subject matter experts and are pleased by the offer to lend a hand.

Talking Points and Guest Presentations

Michelle Beistle, a compliance veteran, observes: "When leaders talk about ethics, people listen. When they don't, people notice."

A lot of leaders truly care about compliance but are simply too busy juggling their own core duties to be able to accomplish what they wish they could with compliance topics. I refer to these folks as the committed but time-poor.

We're so busy with our core compliance duties that we would be stretched to dedicate resources and time to creating awareness about what another department does, right? With that in mind, knowing that there are many leaders who would like to contribute more to tone from the top for the compliance cause, we can help them out by essentially spoon-feeding them assistance.

Remember that this is our day job, the kind of stuff we talk about day in and day out. It's relatively quick for us to rustle up some materials on compliance, and it doesn't preclude the leader from finding a way to make it their own. We are merely providing them with a springboard to leverage.

SAMPLE TALKING POINTS AND QUESTIONS FOR MANAGERS

I just completed the code of conduct/specialized topic training. Who else has completed it? What did you think? Are there any practices we need to reconsider in light of this new/revised policy?

Compliance and senior management ask us to maintain an open-door policy for our teams. What does that mean to you? How can I be better at it?

The employee engagement survey/the company's culture of integrity survey indicates that [X percent] of the organization fears retaliation if they speak up. Any thoughts on why the figure isn't lower? What can I do within our team to get that number down?

Compliance and senior management asks us to promote tone from the top and mood in the middle, meaning that leaders are demonstrably seen to walk the talk about ethics and integrity. What do you think I could do better? What one thing will you do to better walk the talk as a team member?

What do you think is the difference between a culture of integrity and a culture of compliance?

SCAN THIS QR CODE
TO DOWNLOAD +
PRINT A WORKSHEET

You can prepare a list of talking points for managers to help them put compliance on the agenda of their team meetings and make yourself available to chat about them in further detail if required. Here are some examples: The manager confirming that they've taken the recent compliance training and asking if colleagues have any feedback on the training. Reminding their team that their door is always open. Creating an open forum discussion about whether they feel there is psychological safety and a culture of integrity in their department. A recap about the non-retaliation policy. The list is virtually endless.

Pro tip: Offer yourself as a guest attendee if they ever require it. This will permit you an opportunity to present during sales kickoff events and is an excellent way for a leader to show their commitment to compliance. Plus, it's relatively little effort on their behalf — a great win-win.

Incorporating Qualitative Data Analytics Into Your Compliance Training

Your general compliance training covers so many of your staff, you no doubt have other departments hoping to ride on your coattails and asking if you can include a module related to their subject matter in your course. This huge, captive audience is an excellent source of data you can pull from to enhance your compliance program and target remediation or gap areas.

Andrea Falcione from Rethink Compliance astutely points out that so many people get caught up in the idea of data analytics being only about the study of quantitative data. Data analytics certainly can include that type of information, and you should look at it, but not to the exclusion of qualitative data — it's valuable data, too.

I partnered with Rethink Compliance to identify carefully nuanced questions that we considered would give my team in a previous organization a wealth of information to work with not only in regard to our training function but the wider compliance program as well.

Rethink Compliance analyzed the data and provided a report on which business demographics required further education and on what topics. This information informed our training and communications plan for the next year, as well as lots of nuggets of information for other departments. For example, we learned there is an appetite to understand more about the topic of sustainability, so we were able to pass this information to the relevant specialist team.

While I was grateful for the support of a vendor, this is something that you can manage on your own if you wish. The initiative involves crafting a short, prioritized list of survey questions designed to help you pinpoint areas of opportunity in your compliance training or broader program and incorporating it as an element of your annual compliance training.

Then review what the data is telling you and look for specifics, such as whether only one country is struggling with a certain issue, so that you can target any remediation efforts especially to the audience that needs it. To do this, include a question that helps you identify what business unit and/or geography each respondent is from.

We included open text questions as well, so if you go this route, you'll need to be ready to conduct translations in the cases of most international companies and sort through a fair amount of information.

If, like me, spreadsheets and numbers are your kryptonite but you don't have the budget to engage a larger consultancy firm, consider engaging a data analytics intern or new graduate who is more adept in this area and would appreciate some work experience.

Note that sometimes when you receive certain answers, you'll have more questions! Be prepared to establish focus groups to elaborate on certain surprising elements or areas you need to dig deeper on — for example, if you have a large number of staff telling you that they want more education on a topic you've trained on two years in a row, you might need to drill down with more specificity about what it is that people are still confused about.

A lesson I've learned doing this exercise is that instead of holding focus groups, folks have tried issuing another survey in an attempt to be considerate of stakeholder time and allow them to respond at their convenience. Unfortunately, this can be a false economy. If you end up receiving vague responses and don't know who submitted what vague response to follow up again, you're worse off than if you hadn't consulted with the business at all.

Colleagues know that you've sought their opinion and believe that you are going to act on their feedback, but you can't if you don't clearly understand their feedback and have an opportunity to clarify. Way to disestablish trust in compliance! Make sure that if you don't go with a focus group to drill down on the initial information you were provided, you do something else to get specifics, like a one-on-one chat that will give you the opportunity to make sure you really understand what the feedback is and can ask more questions if you need more context and details.

> **Pro tip:** If you're looking for a solution somewhere between 100% DIY and using a vendor, try a tool like Qualtrics, which incorporates automated data analysis features that are not too intimidating, even for folks less than comfortable with figures and spreadsheets (yes, team attorney, I'm looking at and standing right beside you).

Demonstrate the Value of Consultation in Policy Drafting With Cupcakes

Barbara-Ann Boehler, a Massachusetts-based compliance professional, has taught a class on compliance practice skills at Suffolk University Law School for the past several years. Each year, she dedicates one class to an exercise premised on compliance policy development.

For the exercise, the class is divided into two groups. One group is called the "Operations Department" and is given cupcakes, frosting, candy, decorations (and gloves and hairnets). The Operations Department is instructed to frost and decorate the cupcakes. The other group is called the "Compliance Department" and are given the "Code of Frosting Regulations" (CFR). They're instructed to create a cupcake-decorating policy or procedure.

At the end of the exercise, the Compliance Department is asked to read their policy/procedure to the Operations Department, who is asked to validate how the cupcakes were decorated. Without fail, every single time this exercise is run, Barbara-Ann finds that the policy doesn't match the practice because the Compliance Department never consults with the Operations Department.

Those in charge of creating the instructions never think to get the views of the "frontline" individuals who are doing the practical work. It is an eye-opening message and one that won't be soon forgotten thanks to the circumstances of the exercise.

I wish I had known about this exercise earlier in my career. One of the lessons I learned the hard way was that it is better to involve the business as early as possible when drafting policies or rolling out new compliance initiatives. I used to think that it was sufficient to identify a pilot group of staff to roll out a new process or training to first, and then seek feedback and opinions to adjust for the bigger launch. But that's doing the compliance program a disservice. I have realized that I am way better off when I include stakeholders early, as I've espoused elsewhere in this book.

We ask our colleagues to involve compliance early and often. We would do well to give the same courtesy in return.

The cupcake exercise is a truly effective way to get that memorable message off to staff for the rest of their careers. And you'll have dessert sorted for the day!

Frontline Business Staff Drafting Scenarios for Compliance Training

We know that colleagues often prefer scenario-based training where possible. That is consistently the feedback I've received in my data analytics exercises.

It can be difficult to keep coming up with realistic fact-matrix situations, especially for compliance training staff who are in corporate strategic compliance program roles at the global or regional level and don't have interaction and engagement with the front lines in the same way that compliance officers typically do.

Holly Kulka is the global chief risk and compliance officer of a financial services organization. She has found success in inviting frontline staff to submit scenarios for risk topics like conflicts of interest.

This exercise also serves to increase chances of buy-in from the business. When they're included early and often, they're more likely to consider themselves a part of the process, thereby taking responsibility for the initiative, and it's so much harder to challenge something if they came up with it and feel a sense of ownership. They're also in a position to draw any challenges to your attention before the idea is rolled out. This is another way to directly involve senior leadership in the creation of training.

Holly sagely advises, "One good type of training involves a scenario when there are no good answers. We confront that all the time, and of course the answer is not to play ostrich. Usually there is one solution which is significantly better than other solutions, even if not ideal."

We know that the real world often involves shades of gray rather than clear-cut, neatly packaged, model answers. Helping colleagues understand that oftentimes the lesser of a set of evils is the best way forward reflects situations they are more likely to come up against than carefully crafted hypothetical scenarios.

This approach also appropriately respects the intelligence of our colleagues to analyze and think through difficult issues that can, albeit inadvertently, be a problem when we present a patronizing multichoice suite of answers.

Incorporating Adult Learning Theory Into Compliance Training

One of the key tenets of adult learning theory is that learners should have autonomy when being educated. A sense of control and self-direction is important.

A way to encompass these principles in your compliance training is by including a set of several scenarios and the general theme of each one as options. Learners can choose which scenarios to go through as long as they meet your set minimum on each in order to complete the training. For example, you might include five scenarios pertaining to licenses and permits and require learners to complete two of the scenarios of their choosing in order to complete the course.

My former team members Jasper Quak and Lisa-Marie Weber designed a training module very effectively using this approach, and the feedback was overwhelmingly positive.

Time Compliance Initiatives to Coincide with Workforce Presence

Whether qualitative or quantitative, data analytics can be simpler and much more straightforward than you think.

Perhaps the best example of this comes from Andrew Mcbride, risk and compliance leader of a chemical manufacturing company, using common sense to best leverage the attention of his colleagues.

Andrew asked his HR team to help him to identify the day of the year previous where the smallest number of staff took the day off work. This became the day Andrew chose to launch the company's new code of conduct training. This idea can be applied to anything you want to draw attention to with the most attentive and present workforce, such as launching a compliance training module.

Now you may be wondering how to reconcile this with the idea of timing the release of a compliance routine initiative with your annual compliance event, but I've got you covered. First of all, as there's no one-size-fits-all program, there are often several ways to approach your compliance program, and different ideas and rationale will apply to different companies.

Secondly, you can make the two ideas align by using Andrew's approach to identify when you ought to have your compliance week and following on from that, release your compliance training module then.

You can use learning objectives from earlier training modules including the year before for testing on long-term absorption of the content as part of your compliance week activities discussed earlier.

The Next Great Idea: Yours?

Before you started reading this book, you probably had a half-baked idea of something that could solve a problem or speak to a passion starting to take shape in your mind. Maybe you dismissed it as being a bit wacky or thought the world isn't ready for it.

If you were waiting for a sign to put your idea into practice, here I am, lighting a fire under your rump (metaphorically, of course) and encouraging you to get going.

The time is now! While I'd love to be your accountability partner and check in on your progress in a few months, that's not going to be practical.

If you know the fire of motivation may burn out before you finish what you set out to achieve, put an accountability note in your calendar now for three month's time. Tell a friend, family member or colleague what you're doing and when you want to have a deliverable — once you've said it out loud to someone else, it's easier to stick to the commitment and not let it languish by the wayside.

> **"Every revolution was first a thought in one man's mind."**
>
> — Ralph Waldo Emerson

What's stopping you from being a trailblazer?

Living Your Best Compliance Life Outside the Office

It's important to give the best of ourselves to our job and team. It's also critical to think about yourself as a practitioner more holistically and in the context of your wider career and well-being. There is life after your current employer and role! Here are some of my favorite tips for putting your best foot forward beyond your current job.

Keep a notebook detailing your triumphs and accomplishments as you complete projects, segmented by calendar year. This will make completing your performance review documentation easy, as you don't have to stretch to remember details.

But don't throw out the year's worth of notes after your performance review cycle has been completed. This is a treasure trove of information that you can use when you're applying for a new role and need to prepare to answer competency-based questions that ask for you to give an example of when and in what way you have addressed an issue (usually a challenge) previously. For example, "Give me an example of a time where you had to persuade someone to buy into an idea you had for the compliance program."

This notebook will save you from needing to laboriously prepare examples each time you are seeking a new role and can serve as a detailed point of reference when updating your LinkedIn profile and curriculum vitae or resume.

Remember, one of the most common mistakes people make, and I am no exception, when drafting their CV or resume is reiterating their job description instead of focusing on accomplishments and value provided to organizations. Your real-time notes will help you to prioritize some stellar achievements to highlight when you sit down and give careful thought to how you will maximize your value in your CV or resume.

It can be worth filing away your interview preparation for the next job-hunting cycle and simply updating it with new experience and examples, especially with shorter tenures being socially acceptable these days. No point starting from scratch every time, especially if you have some killer examples from earlier in your career.

Establish a wisdom council. Think about people you really admire inside and outside of your company. When you need people to bounce ideas off, seek advice from or simply talk through possible next steps for your career, reach out to your wisdom council.

Think beyond your social and professional circles. If there's someone who is compliance-famous who you think is fabulous but don't know personally, don't be afraid to reach out and let them know what a living legend you think they are to sow the first seeds of friendship.

A decade ago, I was a student of and admirer of Tom Fox from the other side of the world. Fast-forward to today, and he is a producer on the "Great Women in Compliance" podcast, as well as someone I am proud to call a friend.

The best wisdom council relationships have to start somewhere, and the big names in compliance are just mere mortals like you and me. Lisa Fine and I have heard of many success stories where listeners have reached out to guests we've featured on the podcast and mentoring relationships have blossomed. In fact, Lisa and I became collaborators only because she reached out to me after seeing me speak at a conference and we've been friends, and later coworkers, ever since.

Don't forget about diversity on your wisdom council. This group is not the same as a support system, so it's imperative that it not be a multiway echo chamber of only gushing encouragement. Rather, it's what organizational psychologist and author Adam Grant refers to as a challenge network. This is about ensuring the best work is produced, and that means surrounding yourself with different perspectives of people who are not shy to respectfully challenge you and question your work for the purpose of making it better.

In and of itself, the diversity concept could have been part of the main list in this book to remember when hiring for your own team. Like-me bias often results in us hiring people who remind us of ourselves or perhaps our younger selves, people who often share the same background, demographics and physical characteristics. There are countless studies that indicate that a lack of diversity in teams is detrimental to their overall effectiveness.

A previous boss of mine, Mark Stanley, looks to hire people who admirably represent and possess strengths where he has gaps and weaknesses. To take such an approach in building out a team is one of the best leadership lessons I have learned from and believe in. It's a shame in this day and age some people still need to be told we don't need compliance departments full of or necessarily headed by lawyers.

Explore your passions — you never know where they'll take you. Take on hobby or labor-of-love compliance projects outside of your core job in your own time. In addition to the benefits gained in your primary role, which I described earlier, there are broader advantages. Identify something you're passionate about, think about who in your wisdom council also cares about the subject and ask if they'd like to collaborate on it together. This is a way to bring fulfillment and extra exposure to yourself by working on these initiatives and to choose your own colleagues!

Examples of passion projects in which I have built relationships, improved my skill set and gained greater exposure within the compliance community are working on a podcast, being on the planning committee of a conference, collaborating on a panel to speak at a conference, organizing networking meetings, volunteering with a group to support job seekers during the pandemic — the list of opportunities is endless, and there's nothing stopping you from starting up your own project or interest group.

One of my favorite examples of someone who has seized this opportunity is Stan Lui, creating White Hat Guys. What's that project about? I think the tagline says it all: Putting the COOL In COOmpLiance. Stan comes up with innovative compliance communications that really stop people in their tracks because they're so different. An example is an inflatable life ring with the code of conduct documented on it.

And I know the impact of this firsthand. When I was living in Hong Kong, Stan shared one with me; I loved it. He presented these at a company meeting in Kota Kinabalu, Malaysia, an apt setting for visions of lounging in the water. Staff got small ones, while he had a larger one around his waist — difficult not to be intrigued by this display!

Initially, Stan made his ideas available to all in compliance and then later turned White Hat Guys into a side gig. He told me recently with a laugh, "White Hat Guys is for profit now, though not profitable." Good to have a sense of humor about these things! There are opportunities to turn volunteer efforts into side hustles and monetize your hobbies like Stan is doing.

While I am a proponent of sending the elevator back down, that doesn't mean you should spend every moment of your life giving back to others completely selflessly. Take pride in being able to monetize your skill set and ideas, should you decide to do so. A side benefit for Stan, I'm sure, is that all of his efforts also contribute to building his brand in the community as a hard worker and an anything-but-stuffy compliance officer.

As someone who is naturally shy and an introvert, building communities of friends in compliance has helped me come out of my shell and feel comfortable sharing ideas and supporting others. As with Stan, I'm pretty sure it hasn't hurt my personal branding, either. Sometimes personal development is enriched with professional development.

Appreciate colleagues by nominating them for awards. This act of kindness doesn't just benefit the subject of the nomination, but it's been scientifically proven that if you're doling out acts of kindness, you receive benefits, too, such as reduced stress and increased emotional well-being. How's that for a win-win?

Keep a lookout throughout the year for organizations offering recognition in our field or other subject matters that may apply to the exceptional abilities of your colleagues. Remember to include tangible examples to support waxing lyrical about the subject.

The nomination will be judged against many others received, so show why your nominee stands out. Use project examples and data, and get quotes from others where possible so you can make a persuasive case for your nominee.

Before you submit the nomination, make sure you retain a copy of it and send it to the colleague in case they don't get shortlisted so they can hear how grateful you are to be working with them.

This goes for any level. You can and should nominate those reporting to you, peers, allies, supervisors and even your boss' boss. What matters is that in your mind, they fit the bill for the award and you want to see them recognized publicly.

Actions like this not only help your mindful gratitude but also build stronger connections in your network. And you know what they say: Your network is your net worth!

Invest in your personal development. For the most part, we refer to business-related educational opportunities as professional development. However, you can use that new skill set to market yourself for a new role, and when it comes time to leave the organization that paid for your attendance, it's you that retains the knowledge and gets to continue using it in whatever capacity you choose. In that sense, I think it's more apt to call learning new technical skills and gaining knowledge in your craft personal development.

Not every employer will prize upskilling their staff, and for some who do care, the budget simply isn't there to turn interest into action. I have certainly worked for organizations where my boss would sign off on attendance joyously "Only because it's free to attend" and I would not think any more on it, grateful in the knowledge I had found something I could take advantage of.

Now I realize that I was doing myself a disservice and that sometimes it's worth putting personal funds toward new learning opportunities where they are not covered by employers. Many sessions offered without cost are just as good as conferences that come with a registration fee, so keep an eye out for those, but also keep an open mind about the possibility of shelling out personally for desirable opportunities your company may not cover for you.

Even if the budget is not available from your organization, advise your manager that you'd like to attend and cover your own costs. Though you understand the company will not be in a position to share fiscal responsibility, you'd be grateful if they would allow you the time to attend the course.

If money is tight, reach out to the organizer of the conference to say you'd really like to attend but your company is unable to cover attendance and you'll be paying out of your own pocket. Inquire about discounts or other methods of getting you in the door. Perhaps they're still looking for speakers or need a last-minute fill-in for someone who dropped out; these deals usually mean your registration fees are waived.

It always pays to be sincere and ask if there are any other options. There's no shame in prioritizing keeping a roof over your head and the mouths of your loved ones fed. Most conference organizers are thrilled at the prospect of getting more rumps in seats, so they're incentivized to find a mutually agreeable solution.

Closing thoughts

On a cloudy day over high tea at a lovely resort in the desert, my friend Michelle Dewarrat, who heads up a compliance function for a global corporation, was telling me a story about her resourceful son, astutely commenting, "Frustration inspires innovation." I banged my hand a little too hard with enthusiasm on the elegantly set table in agreement, nodding away and saying I needed to incorporate that into this book. She is absolutely correct.

When we are hampered with annoying imperfections, we can either go on doing things the way we've always done them and whine about it, or we can figure out how to make the situation better.

In compliance, if we query a business activity and they respond: "That's the way we've always done it," we usually consider that a red flag. Why should we allow ourselves to succumb to such thinking also?

> *"You never change things by fighting the existing reality. To change something, build a new model that makes the existing model obsolete."*
>
> — Buckminster Fuller

I encourage you not to rest on your laurels and be satisfied with the status quo. Think about what would make us even more effective, what would make our message more impactful and what has worked from your own success stories as well as those of your peers to advance your cause.

I predict that as we invite more learnings from the behavioral science community to inform our initiatives, we'll be more effective and efficient at innovating in compliance. But the ideas and hypotheses have to start somewhere before they can be measured and tested — let them start with you. Read about organizational psychology and other non-compliance specific areas to let seeds of thought germinate, and consider how they can be applied to our work.

My favorite authors in this realm are Adam Grant, Simon Sinek and Malcolm Gladwell. Their books are an excellent starting point to consider how scientific findings about human behavior can impact our compliance programs. Talk to colleagues in your wisdom council and network about what our biggest challenges are currently and what problem-solving has been applied so far to address those issues. What else can you do?

Some other coaching questions to consider:

- What is an idea that was the answer to problems several years ago but might now need to be revitalized or modernized in some way? Take every subelement of your compliance program and critically ask yourself: Am I doing this because it's what we've always done?

- What would great look like?

- Which part of the process or program do colleagues always complain about and why?

- Which part of the process do compliance staff always complain about and why?

- What's something another department in our company does really well in respect to customer service, and how can we best replicate it?

- What bugs me the most about working for my current organization? What control do I have over that?

- If I were to apply disruptive thinking to critiquing my compliance program, what might I discover?

- Can I answer why every piece of my compliance program exists as it is?

- Have I talked to peers about how their compliance program works and asked them what they are most proud of?

- What's my reputation as a compliance officer in this company? How do I know this for sure? How can I check my own perceptions against reality? If my reputation stinks, how can I change that?

- What achievement would look really impressive on my performance review this year? What about when someone asks me about my impact in this company the next time I'm interviewing for a job?

- What's the lowest-hanging fruit we have that is relatively low effort but maximum impact that I can take care of by the end of this month?

- What do I know for sure because I've learned it directly from my stakeholders or other data? What have I been assuming that might be based on mistaken beliefs?

As you come up with the answers to these questions, note them, share connections and solutions with others and let your experiences become another compliance officer's guidebook.

In our quest to evolve and level up, we should also remember our beginnings and our foundations. Michelle Beistle emphasizes that going back to basics is key. I agree. It is important to have the basic elements down and critically review whether we have the cornerstones of our program firmly in place so we don't build on unstable ground.

Ask the fresh eyes joining your team to be honest about what gaps there might be and what their previous employers were doing well.

I know you're busy, but it's a false economy to neglect making yourself aware of developments in the field or priorities of regulators in articles, at conferences and other learning opportunities. Make the time; it's worth it.

In my observations, there is a marked difference between the knowledge of colleagues who actively seek to keep an eye on what is happening in the field and are lifelong learners compared with those who focus on their internal compliance program and their 9-5 job only. I also know which ones I'd choose to work with me in the future if I were to become a hiring manager elsewhere — and it's not the ones who only do the bare minimum.

Consider getting a third-party review every so often from a compliance consultant. Their oversight over numerous compliance programs can be extremely helpful benchmarking knowledge. If you don't have the budget for an overarching review, choose one element of your compliance program this year based on your risk assessment and get another element externally evaluated next year under the new budget.

Similarly, benchmarking reports, often made available by service providers in our space at no cost (you may have to give up personal data like your email address or business phone number) can be useful to understand trends and what others are typically doing with their compliance programs.

Don't get me wrong; you shouldn't jump off a cliff just because everybody else is (hello to all the parents out there), but it certainly is food for thought to see what others are doing and question whether what the majority is doing also makes sense for your program.

A quick internet search should bring up multiple benchmarking reports for you to have a wealth of data to trawl through for comparison purposes. Recording your analysis and own company/program's data against the benchmarking averages and making improvements based on this is helpful for your efforts to incorporate data analytics into planning and implementation for improving your program.

Don't fall victim to compliance officer complacency. Just because you have trained or communicated about something several times doesn't mean that you can close the book on that topic and forget about it. There's no lowest common denominator, and many of the basics need to be tended to as ongoing maintenance.

It is only by having compliance 1.0 in check that we confidently move to compliance 2.0 and the terrain beyond. I am excited about the unknowns and the work we can do to welcome that future. Are you?

Keep living your best compliance practitioner life – happy innovating!

> **"The most difficult thing is the decision to act, the rest is merely tenacity."**
> — Amelia Earhart

ABOUT THE AUTHOR

Mary Shirley *is an international citizen focused on building pragmatic and proportionate compliance programs for multinational corporations and interweaving the values of kindness and sending the elevator back down throughout her personal and professional life.*

She enjoys extreme travel, fashion (including building a carefully curated wardrobe), new cultural experiences, public speaking, sharing good food with friends, talking about anything and everything or when the mood strikes, just sitting in companionable silence in the company of folks with good hearts.

Mary is a strong proponent of carving out dedicated time for rest, relaxation and indulgence, believing that being mindful about allowing yourself these things is the key to living your best life.

"Every now and then, go away, have a little relaxation, for when you come back to your work, your judgment will be surer."

— Leonardo da Vinci